The Unmade Bed
of Architecture

Conversations, Correspondence and other Provocations between Professor Matti K. Mäkinen (Helsinki) and Professor Malcolm Quantrill (Texas) on the theme of Architecture and its Related Culture, published in recognition of Malcolm Quantrill's 50-year involvement in Finnish architecture and culture 1953–2003.

The Unmade Bed of Architecture

Exchanges between
Matti K. Mäkinen and Malcolm Quantrill

Rakennustieto Oy (Building Information Ltd), Helsinki, Finland in association with the Centre for the Advancement of Studies in Architecture (CASA), at Texas A+M University, Texas, USA

RAKENNUSTIETO®

Rakennustieto Oy (Building Information Ltd)
www.rakennustieto.fi
P.O. Box 1004
00101 Helsinki
Finland
phone + 358 9 549 5570

Drawings by Marco Frascari
Photographs: Matti K. Mäkinen pp. 96, 110, 122, 132, 140, 154, 166; Jussi Tiainen p. 120;
Malcolm Quantrill pp. 14, 28, 40, 52, 56, 60, 76, 82, 90, 94, 100, 104, 108, 114, 126, 130, 134, 146, 162, 182, 188;
Pertti Vaasio p. 36

Publisher Rakennustieto Oy (Building Information Ltd)
Language consulting Gareth Griffiths
Graphic design Tuulaleena Hämäläinen
Paper 130 g G Print
Printers Karisto Oy, Hämeenlinna, 2004
ISBN 951-682-761-6

CONTENTS

FOREWORD

Historias Complures Noverit – History and the Search for Invention

Contemporary architectural literature reaches us by means of an exceptionally baffling variety and idiosyncratic modes of writing. Eventually, after extensive sorting and shuffling, these texts may be arranged within a construct that resembles a three-hinged arch; where each hinge corresponds to a different dominant propensity or stylistic approach. Each hinge relates to a different mode of writing that is elaborated to fit into place the characteristics of architecture, considering both the positive and negative sides of our human desire to build. Let me begin by describing the tectonic nature of this arch.

Its structure as an arch form is typified by a hinge at its crown, with two other hinges that connect the arch with its horizontal abutments. This three-hinged arch suffers very little if there are movements in either abutment and adjusts itself to changes in temperature, accommodating expansions and contractions while allowing for asymmetrical movements and variations in loads. Because of its peculiar nature, this type of arch is an ideal diagrammatic, mnemonic device for structuring conversations on the subject of the patterns and forms present in contemporary architectural prose, and the possible consequences they might cast on architectural pleasures. Thus, the three hinges can become vivid for portraying the three dominant modes we find in architectural writing.

Bridging the gap between the ordinary and the extraordinary events that nurture architectural thinking and making, this arch frustrates the present confrontation between pathetically endorsed conceptions of commonplace architecture and the despondently abject views of architectural criticism, together with the fashionable practices of criticism applied to architecture.

An understanding of how this arch maps that conflict and its possible resolution, can be achieved by positioning, what I shall call the "A" and "B" styles of architectural thought that are embodied in the right and left support-hinges. In the "top spot" of this arch, the crown hinge breaks the impassive tectonic palindrome of traditional arches, making it possible to fight the effects of dogmatism: it is here I would locate a third type of architectural thinking and writing that I shall call the "Troubadour Style". This is my recognition of Michel Serres' idea of the "educated thirds", the troubadours of knowledge and their ability to write constructs that can be traced across literature, philosophy, science, mythology and art, their voices breaking through dividing disciplinary walls.

The "A" Style and the "B" styles are characteristic of authors who merely write about architecture by scribbling assessments that are "either/or" commercial and critical reviews of buildings and their edifices, whereas the Troubadour Style is the trait of essayists who dare to write by dwelling within architecture and gamble to write about the "both/and" of its metaphysics and physics.

The major endeavour of "A" style authors is to break up the ontological autonomy of architecture and its superior masterful condition of being a *Regina Virtus*, as it was acknowledged long ago in the sixteenth century by Palladio in the Frontispiece of his *Quattro Libri*, where a titanic lady Mnemosyne always leaves her bed unmade. These authors are partial to a process that restricts architecture's almost unrivalled sovereign condition to stale compartments of academic or professional specializations and taxonomies. Classification is the trademark of the "A" Style in the professional world, whereas historicization is the hallmark of such a style within the walls of academia. In the "A" Style, there is no memory, although its authors claim that they are making history.

The devotees of the "A" style have banished the beautifully coiffed Mnemosyne and her nine gold-crowned daughters, the Muses no less, to a sterile territory marked by a realistic, linguistic and purely relativistic existence that is entirely based on mental constructs. In their impersonal and pseudo-unrhetorical writings, the reality of building which they portray is forced to correspond exactly to the attributes of those mental constructs and these constructs become eternal paradigms that last but a season: these are the invariable, pragmatic specifications that are presently identified as a sustainable, green, deconstructed architecture, or perhaps some bio-architecture combined with other meaningless nominalism.

The "B" style is entirely different. It stipulates that critical modes provide direct illuminations of architecture rather than the opposite, and that those illuminations are conveyed through a search for uniqueness. The thinkers working within this writing style want to carry out an ontological deregulation of all architectural categories and to breed such new ones as "blobs," "contextures" or "phylums." They spread unpleasantly cold consecrations throughout the architectural field. They do not set any intrinsic harmony between architecture and intelligence. They see the public exercise of architecture as an alteration, an estrangement of intelligence, an instance of stellar inhumanity and of forced conceptualism.

Two architects, a Finn and an Englishman, come together here in a series of conversations and other encounters, intent on confronting the present condition of architecture. Professor Matti K. Mäkinen enjoyed prominence in his career as an architect in Helsinki, as a designer, as a strategist and as an administrator. He was Director-General of Rakennushallitus (The National Board of Public Building) from 1985 to 1994, having the distinction of being the last in a notable lineage. Although he retired at the end of 1994, Mäkinen continues to worry about the condition of the architectural profession and architectural education, raising his voice with other international scholars in a chorus that might, in the spirit of the late Reima Pietilä and *The Beatles*, be thought of as *The Arctic Long-Day's Night*.

According to the Law of Sublime Coincidence, Malcolm Quantrill began his involvement in the Finnish ethos during the summer of 1953 when, as a young student, he was employed in that same architectural office of Rakennushallitus, that was to become Mäkinen's centre of influence.

At the outset of this project, Mäkinen collaborated with Roger Connah to invent the form of these exchanges, translating them into a vigorous structure of debate that springs adroitly from foundations of mere casuistry to the high vaults of speculation. With sensitivity and incisive analytic perceptions, Mäkinen positions the "A" and "B" styles firmly on their appropriate abutments, taking the full thrust of Quantrill's "Troubadour Style" and allowing it to flourish as a freely centred third hinge of the arch, accommodating the full expression of his inventive provocations in the field of architectural theory.

This Troubadour Style is the blueprint of a dynamical system that sorts out in asymmetry the confrontation between the "B" and "A" styles. It is a veritable bulldozer fuelled by memory, a powerful piece of equipment which can remove the rubble from the one side and tear down the forest on the other side, thereby allowing the construction of new edifying architectures. These troubadours are crucial figures among architectural writers, in and for our time, since they configure knowledge and work the memories of the past into the future.

Malcolm Quantrill draws on the propensity of the Troubadour Style in his transactions with architectural theory, successfully reconstructing the connection between architectural representations and cultural experiences, tastes and mentalities by locating architectural instances that are embodied in the everyday and putting them *sub specie aeternitatis*. Quantrill's style is surprisingly involved in detecting micro-events, everyday sayings and perceptions that connect the narratives of architectural making with the chronicles of non-architecture, raising unexpected outcomes. His considerations and epistolary conversations are a powerful contrivance by which he brings to light how ordinary procedures of building and thinking about building become generally misconstrued in their inherent poiesis and how this results in bodiless architecture.

Writers working within the Troubadour Style proceed in a non-aligned manner. They use a contemplative, reflective manner that helps them to evoke explicative tropes. The word *troubadour* comes from the Occitan verb "trobar" meaning 'to find, to invent, to compose' and *trobar* derives from Latin *tropare*, to compose tropes.

In the first of his ten books, Vitruvius sets out his prescription for architectural education, saying: "Histrorias complures noverit". This is generally translated as "knowing history", but in reality the participle "*noverit*" means not merely to know but also denotes a search for an innovative telling of events by bringing wonder into the equation. Wonder is a faculty that has completely disappeared from contemporary architectural discourse and is today realized only by accident. The word wonderful is almost meaningless, an expression of praise and celebration, used to avoid deeper and more specific comment, but Quantrill tells us wonderfully innovative stories which are Ariadne's clues spun from cultural and social yarns, which can lead us in turn out of our present mazes of architectural thinking and making.

Memory in the form of asymmetry and symmetry always constitutes the absence of memory. Symmetry makes impossible to distinguish transformational events. For example, a circle is the most symmetric figure and any of its rotated versions is indistinguishable from the initial one. Asymmetry reveals memory by incorporating the past in the picture. Memory can take many forms. For example, a *scar* is memory of preceding actions because, when we look at it, we are able to extract *information about a past injury, a wound, a cut through* the skin as forensic science teaches us. For Norwegian architect Sverre Fehn, making architecture is a dramatic event that represents the interpretation of "A Cut, a Wound and a Bandage".

Again, a *fissure* in a wall is a memory of past events because, when we look at it, we are able to extract *information about past actions*, e.g., that the foundation had settled. There are, in fact, an almost infinite number of asymmetric forms that function as memory: scars, fissures, dents, injuries, intensifications, diminutions, unmade beds, messy dinner tables and so on. In the troubadour style these asymmetric forms – e.g., Kristian Gullichsen's definition of architecture as being either an elephant or a butterfly – take place within a *relational* way of knowing. With respect to the past, such a way of knowing recognizes the incorporation of historical subjects and attends to the materiality of the evidence they have left behind, and at the same time acknowledges the incorporation of the writer in the face of that evidence.

The Troubadour Style is evocative, but at the same time it is demanding and rather difficult to perform. This difficulty is partly related to the rigour with which the arguments and demonstrations of ideas must be constructed. They are a delicate blend of culture, nature, science, the arts and humanities, and require a finely balanced selection of ingredients that must be *stirred* rather than shaken, to achieve the perfect *Dry Martini.*

Architectural troubadours believe in the potency of their findings to subvert fixed, steady and stale knowledge, by enacting transitions across space and time without teleological purposes. These troubadours are not rebellious radicals but the whisperers of a perpetual contestation that ignores specific polemics and arranges a line of defence around the essential elements of our understanding and representation of the world. The troubadours of architecture defeat and disperse into rejection every abuse made of reason by the duplicity of the languages used in populist architectural markets or in elitist critical practices.

Malcolm Quantrill is unquestionably a real troubadour of architectural knowledge. He knows how to tell architectural stories in a novel way, but at the same time he is able to illuminate essential points of reference within the sphere of architectural theory.

Marco Frascari, Professor and Director
School of Architecture
Carleton University, Ottawa, Canada
August, 2004

1

BALTHUSIAN DILEMMA

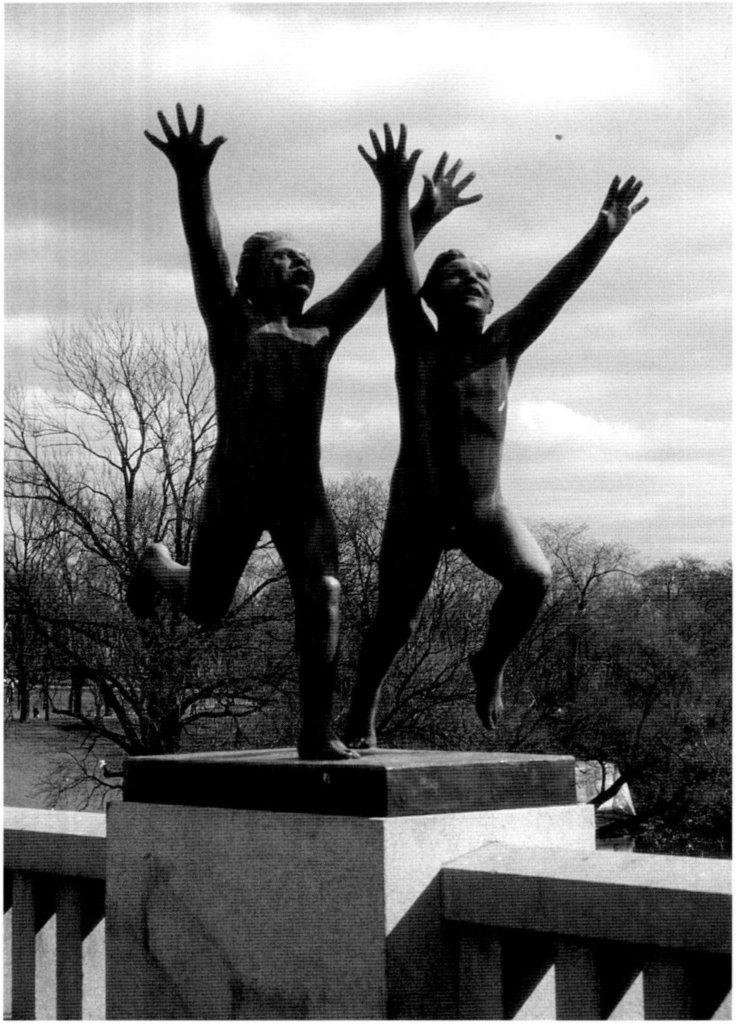

COUNTERPOINT | Malcolm Quantrill – Matti K. Mäkinen

MQ: One afternoon, in the spring of 1955, Louis Kahn asked his graduate class at the University of Pennsylvania: "Please tell me what you think architecture is?" Total silence ensued. Not one of us dared answer this philosophical provocation. Eventually, Kahn broke the silence and told us: "Architecture is the essential repetition of essentials". He went on to explain that: "These essentials consist of number, of rhythm, of harmony, of proportion, of coherence, of poetry, of the relationship of the parts to the whole". He concluded: "This essential repetition makes up the Body of Architecture". Hence the "Body" in my titles.

MKM: To present and re-present. Like Karsten Harries puts it: "Architecture is an art of representation". Since the Modern Movement has stopped long ago, the modern has frozen to an "ism", producing re-re-re-presentations, seemingly empowered by a renewable energy.

MQ: Kahn was himself repeating the basic construct of our building art *(Baukunst)*, the repeated element that gives both essential form and desirable variety to the architectural presence.

MKM: The need to use the German word *Baukunst* suggests one definition for architecture: the art of building. Which turns the question of the essence of architecture to questioning the essence of art. Following that path, instead and before defining the art of building, we have to define art *per se.*

MQ: Architecture, like poetry, has not only form and content, but also cadence, rhythm and the of elements. Architecture is the continuing invention (or reinvention) of itself.

MKM: Is this why the Goddess of Architecture sometimes behaves so capriciously? How about us humans, are we capable of a continuous self-renewal?

MQ: Wait a moment...let's stick to architecture for a while. Andrea Palladio did not know what a "country villa" was! But he was able to invent it out of architecture. Palladio's poem of the country villa tells the story of *new* architectural experiences in classical terms that would have still been familiar to the villa owners. The elements of architecture, like the recognisable bits in a fairy tale, recur in the Palladio story, but it is his unique way of telling the classical tale.

MKM: As to Palladio's poem, we can also make a note of recent developments where Gaston Bachelard's "Poetics of Space" has become the favourite reading among young architects and students.

MQ: What, then, is the secret of this story telling? Is it the secret of all lasting (enduring - like, for example, Rossi's *permanences)* stories, the great folk-tales. Ludwig Wittgenstein observed that: "Architecture immortalises and glorifies something. Hence, there can be no architecture where there is nothing to glorify"; to which Colin St John Wilson adds: "Where there is no necessity there can be nothing to celebrate". Does this mean that when he is confronted by a folly, what Wilson sees is for him something less than architecture? I would rather believe that architecture exists to celebrate our sense of *play* just as much as obedience to *function*..

MKM: Maybe this *play* dimension should be counted as one of the functions in architecture. To be an object of art, a presence – *ein Gegenstand* – needs an author and this author must act with the intention of making art. The play needs a playwright. The intentional dimension gives some enlightenment to the mystery of architecture. To be a piece of architecture, a building needs a creator who has the intention of making architecture. In building, this is not always the case.

MQ: The act of story telling, and the folk-fairy tales themselves, are an essential part of cultural memory. They remember certain truths and myths that reside in our *being.* Through repetition, these stories penetrate to our innermost consciousness. The story-telling of architecture also builds a structure of cultural continuity. Architecture remembers time and events, immortalising and glorifying them: it also remembers itself in its own continuous reinvention.

MKM: Roland Barthes, in his *Mythologies* (1957) declares nature as the common denominator of myths. A myth is a story that tries to find a sustainable, eternal, "natural" explanation to a historical phenomenon. But then, in a way of seeking distance to nature, Barthes writes, how ... "the most elevated form of artistic expression is a near by alphabetical interpretation, finally some kind of algebra. All forms should strive after abstraction, which in no way conflicts elegance."

MQ: Perhaps this is what Louis Kahn also had in mind, as though he were describing the essential elements of a story, because the architectural story parallels the literary form in this respect. After all, architecture is a similitude of poetry and the poetic dimension. Architects are constantly inwardizing images, structures, rhythms and cadences, then repeating these elements to themselves as they form and reform a narrative, a sonnet, a *haiku,* in space and time.

MKM: In her diploma thesis, a Finnish student of architecture points out, that "poetry and architecture are bound together by counterpoint, undefinability and abstraction of nature elements". I have understood that in music teaching the idea of Counterpoint includes the assumption that every student has a voice. Most traditional instruments are designed to sing, that is to say to imitate the voice, and instruments are much more varied in construction and idiom than voices.

MQ: Without an *appetite* for a tale, a song, a poem, we cannot recognize the cadence and rhythms of our existence in time and space. We need the capacity, the cultivated sensitivity to inwardize the prosody of those narratives. Without such inwardizing we cannot tell our own stories, and this means that we cannot take part in the continuing poetic of literature and architecture. When we lack the capacity to inwardize, when we are deprived of such participation, we will fail to grasp conceptual ideas about the meaning of form, space and content – of *being* itself.

MKM: Why don't we leave the last word to Daniel Libeskind. He has defined *genius loci* by stating that "space is actually something like a person, a physiognomy, a soul, a spiritual entity given to a particular locale. And that's the *genius loci* we feel when we are in a place."[1]

[1] Daniel Libeskind, "Where are we now?", *Architectural Record,* 03/2003

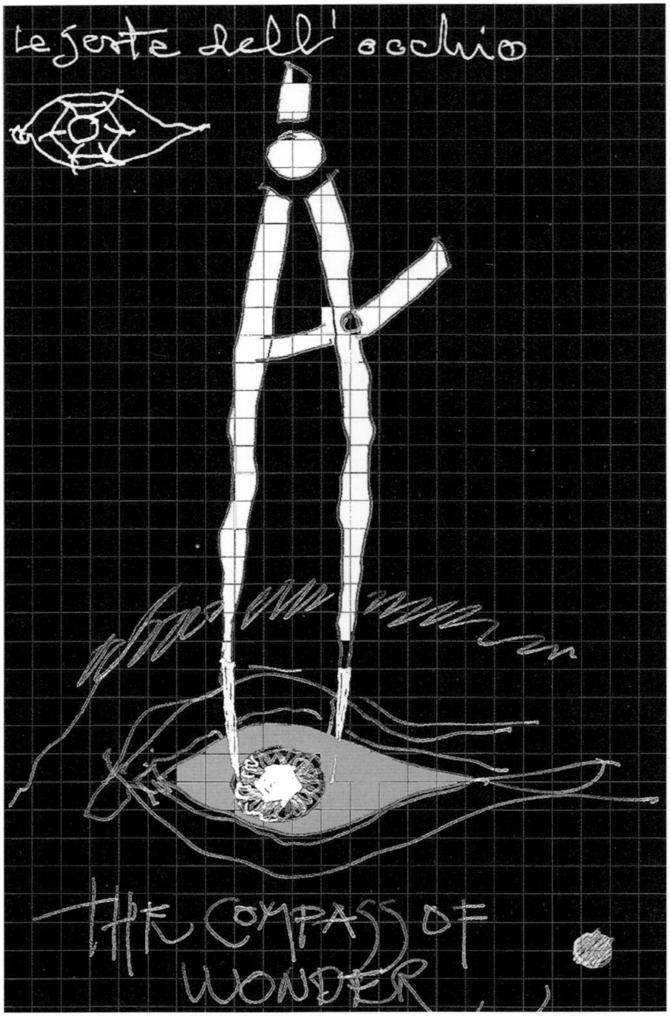
Le gerte dell' occhio
THE COMPASS OF WONDER

PREPARING FOR DESIGN | Matti K. Mäkinen

While trying to discover the idea behind this title, I recall three occasions from my past when I had to address schools of architecture at the celebrations of their respective anniversaries. Those were the Technical University of Budapest (200 years old in 1983) and in Finland at the departments of architecture in Oulu University and Tampere University of Technology a few years later. Here, I am going to jump out of those "pulpits" to take a look at the present.

Is architecture tired?

A friend's health had failed dramatically, leading to a severe crisis. He had to face the ultimate questions. After the time spent in hospital, nothing seemed the way it used to be. The roads now seemed blocked, instead he felt a strong need for a thorough renewal.

They speak of a crisis in architecture. This is certainly not just idle talk and theorizing, which passes by an ordinary architect, busy at his desk, without his noticing. Scarcely any one of us has avoided a situation where the drafting hand hesitates and a nagging doubt takes over.

The architect has maybe more clearly than ever arrived in a situation which carries all the signs of a battlefield. On the one hand he can be a Hamlet, questioning the meaning and justification of his existence, on the other he resembles the brave Don Quijote, hastening towards those ghostly, churning windmills. And if we look back just a few decades, the built world we have inherited seems to give the impression of an idyllic era when our colleagues worked in an atmosphere of positive interest and esteem. No one questioned the value or necessity of the architect's work. Good achievement was rewarded by respect and a decent income. The clients and the architects had shared values. It was easy to adopt a common language of expression and within that framework we could tell the valuable from the worthless.

Pure white discipline...

I won't repeat the whole speech I gave in Budapest two decades ago. Here, I will only take up some of the points I tried to make. As a background – and a backbone – in an architect's professional work, I mentioned technical and social problems of construction, which looked as though they had been solved forever. As a result a firm discipline was born, easy to adopt and teach to the new generations of architects.

...and the diaspora

We know how the story goes on. Functionalism has fallen and the modern movement split apart. The right manifests have somehow given us a wrong world. And the personifications of the Right Faith, the original prophets, have left this world, are no longer with us. In the disturbed times that followed, many minor prophets have put up their road-signs, showing the way to all possible and impossible directions. And still worse, we stand here, saying, like *Alice in Wonderland: "If you don't know where you want to go, it is all the same which way you take."*

The uncertainty, as reflected in our professional behaviour, has weakened our position as potential leaders of the building process. We have lost the ancient role of High Priests of construction, as supreme builders. New leaders from other professions are eagerly taking over, bringing with them their own attitudes and professional beliefs. A blind *materialism* has become so commonly accepted that the 'soft' values, already *par definitio* belonging to architecture, have been made more morally dubious.

These new high priests have extended the claim of exact knowledge even into the realm of architecture. This phenomenon has been fortified by a multitude of standards and jurisdiction. We need standards to guarantee health and safety, for a good life in a good environment. We need standards to take into account the technical, economic and ecologic aspects. We need standards to deal with sudden, surprising, mysterious or symbolic occurrences. We need standards to expel the art from architecture.

As teachers, we are today preparing architects for the next millennium. What can be our message to them today? That was already my question in 1983, two decades ago.

What can we tell them?

In a detailed conclusion, I drew attention to some key concepts. To make it short, I will mention here only the following:

– Throughout the history of civilization, there has always been Architecture.

– There is always an architect for all kinds of building tasks. If he is not called by this title or specially trained to do the job, somebody else will take his place. This somebody will then be the real architect. He will say the last word.

– For an architect, the most important mental capital is *idealism*, based on an honest search for answers to human needs.

– The *values and attitudes*, based on this idealism, still bring together all the architects in the world. How these values are submitted in the course of architectural education, belongs to the eternal mysteries of architecture.

– Last but not least, I mention the *visionary* essence of the profession. Knowledge and vision, both are needed. But much more valuable than knowledge is *understanding*.

– In this expert-crowded world of ours, we have too many right answers to wrong questions. What is essential, therefore, is an ever ongoing search for the *right questions*.

Preparing for Design

Now, twenty years after I uttered the above definitions, what would I like to change or make afresh?

Not much, really. I believe I would not remove anything; just compress everything into a shorter chapter to create space for some new features that have occurred in the more recent past. These phenomena can be divided into two groups, those concerning the contexts of architecture and those concerning architecture itself.

The context....

A short list of contextual changes that deserve closer study might be viewed as follows:

– Prevailing concepts of the market economy have visible impacts on the ethics and aesthetics of architecture and the architectural profession.

– The hidden client moves his investments from here to there, and there are migration movements of workers in search of jobs and welfare as a result.
– Among those who can afford to buy, a consumer frenzy quickly develops.
– The concept of the information society, with its cross-influences on man both as an individual and as a group, on the mind as well as the body, not to mention its impact on human culture in all its forms prevails.
– Preparations for Disasters, due to widely differentiated developments, symbolically accentuated through the September 11th terrorist massacre in New York are accompanied by the diminishing possibilities of finding individuals willing to take care and responsibility for other people and their lifeworld.

The list above offers just a few hints towards directions where you could try to look behind the mirror of architecture. And who looks back but Life itself, "the way of life of our period" (Giedion).

...and architecture

What, then, could be said about architecture itself, to provide some instructive material for architects of the future? A short list again might give some ideas of what I have in mind. Could these be some of the 'right' questions?
– What kind of design would you prepare for (or sell to) an unknown user or an anonymous client? A real estate agent or an unknown investor, an invisible client hidden far away far away along the production chain? Somebody who has never visited the site and has no other interest but a monetary one?
– What kind of innovations can you present when your task is fitting together readymade fragments produced by the material industry in different parts of the world?
– How do you feel about the ecology of taking the raw materials, the long-range criss-cross transportations of the parts and pieces for you to put it together, and blow the spirit of architecture in this heap of this and that?
– How do you pay respect to the *genius loci* and create added value to your site and the community around, other than the rising price of real estate?
– How do you prepare for disasters of different kinds? What is your interpretation of sustainable building? How do you build for need and not for vanity or waste?

In conclusion

These are only a few examples of the 'right' questions. My last advice for any future architect is that it is *you* who should concentrate in finding the questions. This is why I did not mention the all enfolding Information Society with its unimaginable consequences to come. These you have to see – or rather foresee – and act accordingly. That constitutes the threshold to a new Renaissance of Architecture.

It is more important to know who you are than where you are going, because where you're going will change as the surrounding world changes.[1]

[1] See Collin-Porras, "Building Your Company's Vision", *Harvard Business Review of Change,* Harvard Business School Press, Cambridge, Mass., 1998.

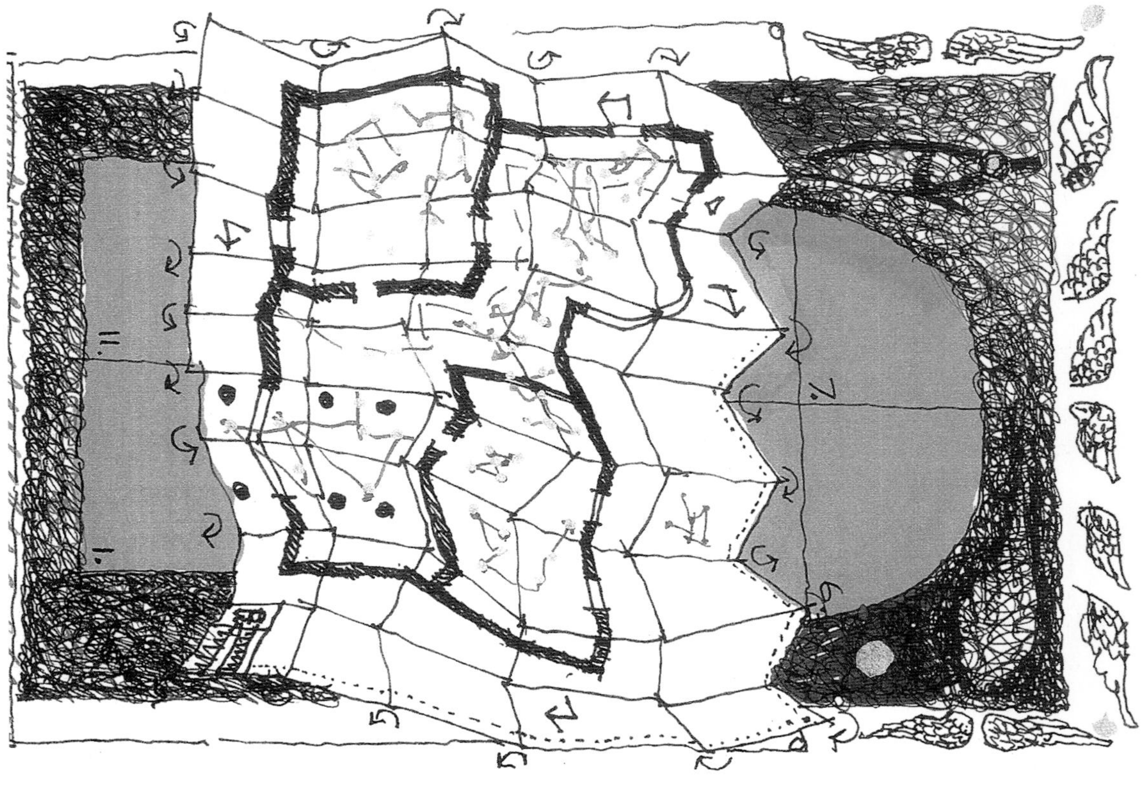

DRAWING FROM THINKING TO BUILDING

Malcolm Quantrill

The idea for this provocation – *Drawing from Thinking into Building* – has three sources. First were the demonstrations quoted by Marco Frascari in his lecture at Texas A+M in the autumn of 2003 – namely those provocative and haunting drawings made for The New Yorker by architect Saul Steinberg. These show, among other things, how on the front cover of that magazine, in the span of just a few inches, you could have your imagination stretched from 9th Avenue in New York City to San Francisco and the Pacific Ocean. Steinberg therefore offers a prime example of how the draughtsman is not merely in the business of recording; he is also actually involved in the process of "drawing from thinking into building". In other words, Steinberg "builds" an image that does not and could not actually exist in space. His drawings are not records of existing fabrics; they are therefore what I call, in the spirit of Johann Sebastian Bach, Steinberg's "two-part inventions".

Frascari's lecture was followed by the first architecture debate of the year, in which I built on Finnish architect Kristian Gullichsen's provocative question: "Is Architecture an Elephant or a Butterfly?" In our discussion, Professor B provided our second source in her account of an episode while teaching at the University of Texas. She had been allocated a teaching assistant, an overseas student who had almost no English, and Professor B was having nightmares about the impact, or lack of it, this assistant would have on her undergraduate students.

But the saving grace of this almost-dumb helper was his superb skill as a draughtsman. Whenever a serious question came up in the studio he would take a large sheet of paper, sit cross-legged on the floor and use his big, soft pencil to carry on a dialogue with the students. The result, Professor B told us, was "quite splendid". So, a young man, who was severely handicapped in his speech turned out to be a star performer through his special skills as a draughtsman.

The third source comes from the work of the nineteenth century French theorist, Eugene Viollet-le-Duc, who divided the processes of architectural education – and therefore *dessin* or "drawing" – into two main parts. In our present-day terms, these were:

(1) The study of architectural history and theory for the purpose of understanding the principles of the planning, structure and composition of historic buildings.

(2) The analysis of contemporary (i.e. the "present-day" of the time in which the student/architect lives and works) buildings, and the interpretation of knowledge of previous ages; the purpose being to understand how that knowledge may relate to or be applied in solving contemporary architectural problems.

Viollet-le-Duc remains an important theorist today because he deviated substantially from the theory taught at the École des Beaux Arts. The École predicated that historic examples should be directly applied to the solution of New Architecture. The result was that the New Architecture of the École des Beaux Arts could not de facto be new at all, because it depended upon actually COPYING the Old Architecture. Viollet-le-Duc's thesis required students and architects not to copy but to analyse historic precedents, establishing universal principles that can then be referenced as underpinnings for new designs.

In this sense, too, Viollet-le-Duc, opposed direct "drawing from the cast", which was the quintessential copyist technique of the École des Beaux Arts, but the development of an understanding of the object being studied (building or sculpture). In other words, Viollet-le-Duc called upon the student or architect to "draw from thinking (about the object)". And "thinking about something" is another way of talking about its analysis.

Just in case three sources are not enough to get our creative juices working, I'll end by quoting from a book we published here at Texas A+M University in January, 2003: *The Architectural Project* by Alfonso Corona-Martinez, a Professor from Belgrano University in Buenos Aires. On the first page he puts us straight about the role of drawing in our thinking and making architecture. He says:

"Design is the invention of a new object through the mediation of another object that precedes it in time. The designer operates on this, the project, modifying it, confident that it is satisfactory. Then its characteristics are translated into a code of instructions that can be understood by those in charge of realizing the second object – known as 'the work' or building."

Corona-Martinez tells us that there are two factors that condition the specification and representation of "the object" or "the work", which are:

(1) The separation of designers and executors, which began in the Renaissance. He quotes Richard Neutra: "...drawings and blueprints are a rather recent development. In past periods, the originator of a design usually communicated his ideas directly to his working crew, clarifying it by showing them what to do."

(2) The actual need for a design arises, and in the attempt to design and realise this "object", the designer investigates the greater or lesser degree of novelty compared to others already existing in the same "class", in other words, its proximity to a known "type".

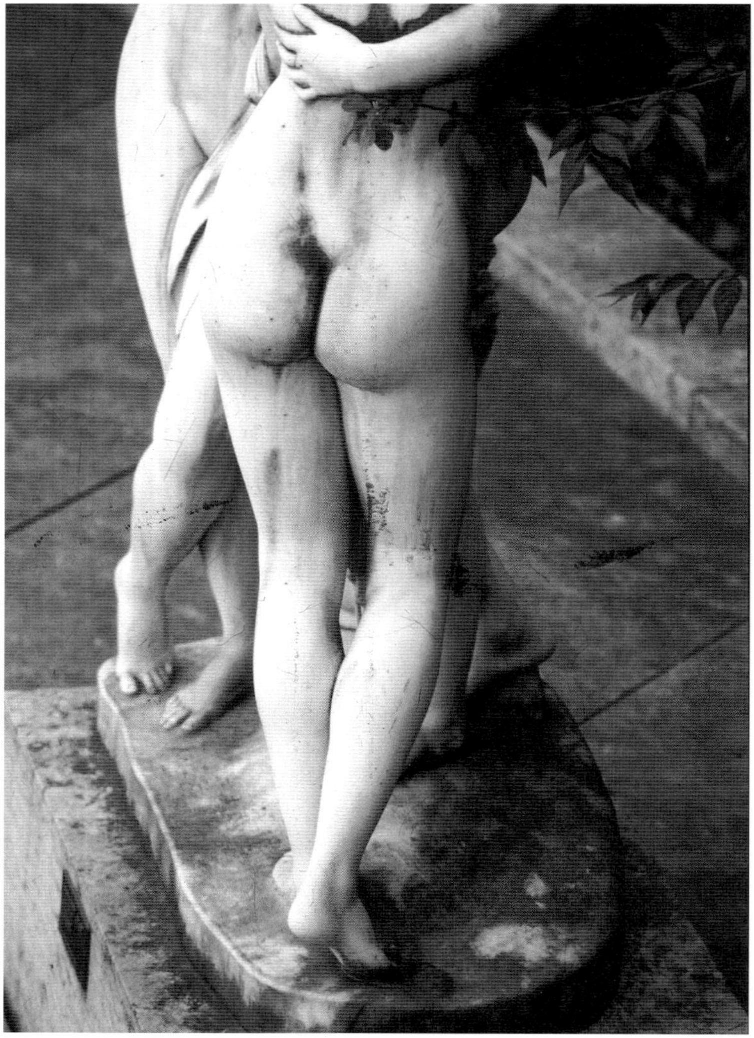

ARCHITECTURE AS A BALTHUSIAN DILEMMA

Malcolm Quantrill

"Why don't we talk about what art really is? It's a skill like that of an artisan or a farmer. We need it for such tasks as making a hole in the ground. A certain physical effort is always required to realize the goals we set ourselves. It is a way of discerning hidden secrets, as well as deep and distant paths, that are quite inaccessible and timeless."

Balthasar Klossowski[1]

This text summarizes my recent explorations in architectural theory (1998 – present). In broad terms, my focus has been on the relationship between architecture and the socio-cultural framework that conspires in its conception and realization. My researches were prompted by a number of stimuli, both real and abstract, involving new entities, and causing me to change direction in pursuit of architecture's contradictory hypotheses.

In 1969, the American architect Robert Venturi attempted to redefine Architecture as residing in the metaphors of "either a duck or a decorated shed". I offer here my own proposal that:

"Architecture represents the characteristics of *either* a BOX or those of a MUSICAL INSTRUMENT: In the first case presenting a rigid, inflexible form, and in the second positing an open framework that permits fingering which leads to performance and interpretation".

My theory examines the nature of architectural concepts in terms of their real and perceived identities: I try to make the Art of Architecture – *Baukunst* – that can be better understood by educated people. Given the choice between an inflexible, silent BOX and the *poetic, lyrical potential* of an INSTRUMENT, we may understand the architect's Balthusian Dilemma. The elephantine mass of Architecture has already failed to survive. While the frail, evenescent *lepidoptera* cannot, alas, "take like a duck to water".

[1] The Polish artist known as "Balthus" (1908–2001)

At the Symposium sponsored by Princeton University School of Architecture in 1990 the opening paper was given by feminist Meaghan Morris. It dwelt upon an exposure of aspects that centred on an early cinematographic myth, that of King Kong. This fictional jungle primate, made larger than life with the aid of Hollywood's special effects technology, was presented as conquering space in the Big City (originally New York, but translated to Sydney in the hands of the Australian Ms Morris) by climbing and taking possession of its tallest tower. The tower in question was not an example of modernist architecture. Indeed, it has to be emphasized here that the modernist tower is far from being a common architectural occurrence.

Now, we return to Morris's paper, provocatively titled: "Great Moments in Social Climbing", and her interest in the domain of verticality with its implications of male sexuality in architecture.

As a feminist, Morris naturally seeks to interest us in the quality of "difference" in its various aspects. Specifically, in terms of the sexual significance of towers, she stresses the importance of our understanding the *difference* between: (A) an investment of male ego. Man-efests in architectural terms the dominant verticality inherent in male sexual organs; and (B) its symbolic representation of the male organ as a mere *phallus*.

On the one hand we have an investment of male ego in the formal representation of male sexual power as a vertical construction more normally thought of as "erection"; on the other hand we are confronted by a mythic memory or translation of that power into a symbol of implied sexuality. In other words, a tower cannot itself represent the male sexual organ, because it is not a primary signification of sexuality at all; but through its transformation into what we term "high-rise" its otherwise *Real Estado* suggests a decidedly sexual interpretation.

First, we have the power and persuasion of original Freudian symbolism; then comes the inevitable blending of symbol with Classical myth; with the consequence that the action shifts to the realm of what we might term the "troubador phallus". Inevitably, the darker side of dreams and myth perverts the course of human love by introducing a draftsman's aid, a "facilitator", the post-nursery toy known as a dildo (a term of unknown origin, but possibly stemming from Australia, where it describes an abbreviated form of the tubular Aborigine *didgeridoo;* or linked to the *Ersatz peni* much favoured by German scientists). It can also be used to describe: (a) a stupid or despicable person; and (b) the "dildo tree", a tall, vertical and ribbed species of West Indian cactus, known to Westerners through its use in a Caribbean infusion known as a "sticky-fix". This concoction is believed by a number of prominent psychiatrists to induce a state of *Ersatz-Erlebnis* or "false experience". In Texas, it is simply not possible without celebrating the presence of its cactus strains, those prevailing image of its structure, its vigorous triumph over its environment, its durability in resisting what can only be described as Nature's worst tricks, and finally the sublime coupling of a thorny masculine epiphany with its feminine delicacy yet persuasively seductive *flora.*

We have gone full circle in the company of Ms Morris, tracing the idea of the tower as a symbolic representation of the male organ through to its displacement as a mere "dildo". This has the effect of reducing the significance of a modern tower from a full-blown sexual symbol of male sexuality to that of a toy-phallus, a mere plaything in the architect's hands. And since all sex-play attracts social and moral stricture, Ms Morris may be credited with hastening the extinction of what was already a rare species – the Modernist Tower.

In the vast ocean of counter-currents and confusion that has characterized much Post-Modernist criticism, Laura Mulvey's paper "Pandora: Topographies of the Mask and Curiosity" has the virtues of being brief, to the point, and engaging immediately with architectonic relationships. She opens by referring to Gaston Bachelard's *The Poetics of Space* (New York, 1964). The connection between Bachelard and the infamous "box" of Pandora is immediately apparent. After Prometheus angered the Gods of Ancient Greece by stealing their fire, the Gods "designed" Pandora as their "avenging angel" and sent her on her mission with a box full of trouble. Literally manufactured by the god Vulcan, Pandora is an early example of the robotic type. At the same time, like Eve in the Garden of Eden (and in a somewhat similar scenario), Pandora is, according to Greek mythology, the first mortal manifestation of woman. Marina Warner, in her study *Monuments and Maidens* (London, 1985) provides this assessment of Pandora's attributes: "… a most subtle, complex, and revealing symbol of the feminine, of its contradictory compulsion, peril and loveliness; … artifact and artifice herself, Pandora installs the woman as the *eidelon* (idealized image) in the frame of human culture, equipped by her unnatural nature to both delight and deceive."

Mulvey stresses the "dislocation between Pandora's appearance and her meaning", suggesting that: "She is a Trojan horse, a lure and a trap, a *trompe l'oeil.* Her appearance dissembles her essence. The very attraction of the visible surface suggests an antimony, a 'dialectics of inside and outside'" (Bachelard).

Thus, the architectural context is quite clearly defined. We see that here we are dealing, in Brunelleschi's terms, with the difference between *substance* and *appearance.* Mulvey's reference to the Trojan horse confirms that, in Pandora's case, things are not what they seem. This *difference* applies equally to Pandora and to her box: that is, the missile is a bearing from the Gods. In both cases the exterior form belies the contents. My use of "cases" is deliberate, because both Pandora and her box are deceptive containers of "otherness". The architectural implications of such containment and what is contained are obvious, but it is important to differentiate here between the box-like box we associate with Pandora – i.e. Pandora's Box as the container of all the World's ills – and Pandora herself as a unique representation of female being in the mortal world. To that purpose she had been hammered out and cast by Vulcan in his forge, assuming the form of an alluring "body", endowed with charm, beauty, cunning and deception, making her the original *femme fatale*. But with all these virtues and vices she remained a mere container: an exquisitely inlaid Damascus-box, perhaps, but a box nevertheless.

In fact, the box originally assigned to Pandora was in the form of a ceramic jar, a much less portable container. During the inventive Early Renaissance period, however, this larger vessel was shrunk down to a box which Pandora could carry in her hand[2]. In any case, this Greek myth has never been known as "Pandora's Jar", but the translation from jar to box is typical of those provocative Renaissance adaptations of Classical formal and spatial values.

In part this translation of form derives from a desire to simplify. The original formula allows two "vessels", the one being the manufactured body of Pandora and the other her pottery jar. When the jar is shrunk and reconstructed as a box, Pandora's body, too, loses its art form and resumes the constructed box form consistent with Vulcan's production techniques. We have noted, in the case of both Pandora and her box, that there is a conflict of outer appearance with interior contents. We know only what we can observe the exterior form of the container, while what is concealed within remains a hidden secret.

Mulvey quotes Ludmilla Jordanova[3]: "'Veiling' implies secrecy. Women's bodies, and, by extension, female attributes, cannot be treated as fully public, because something dangerous might happen, certain secrets be let out, if female bodies and attributes were simply left open for all the world to see. Yet in presenting something as inaccessible and dangerous, an invitation to know and to possess is extended. Secrecy associated with female bodies is sexual and linked to the multiple associations between women and privacy. Conversely, when a female 'box' is opened up, the secrets it formerly concealed are disclosed and consequently become public knowledge."

Clearly, there are two *different* conditions of privacy relating to Pandora: the one secreted within her own female container (originating from Vulcan's workshop) and the other locked up in her

[2] Dora and Irwin Panofsky, Pandora's Box, 1956
[3] Sexual Visions, 1989

mysterious box of tricks. It is important to demonstrate the significance of this double standard of female secrecy, and show its relationship to the process of architectural creativity. For this purpose we shall consider Pandora's "box of tricks" as the archetype of all provocation and manipulative seduction, of all artifice and simulation of aesthetic attraction.

On this basis we can now reconsider our two boxes in terms of their limitations. A "Body of Knowledge" box is a resource for creative strategies of seemingly infinite capacity; while a portable "box of tricks" is a closed and finite container whose contents are consequently limited by its physical dimensions. To activate the "Body of Knowledge" it would appear necessary to treat it as an instrument capable of fine tuning, a keyboard to be brought into syncopation, strings to be teased in search of harmony.

Once opened the "box of tricks" reveals all its contents, including the limitations of preliminary design strategies. In this sense Pandora's box is a throw-away, for its inner secrets once disclosed will be displaced by subsequent ideas and developments. Once Pandora's Box has been discarded, the architect can take up the body or "instrument" of Pandora herself, and prepare to engage in the composition of a new and unrestricted work. There would therefore appear to be a *difference* between "Pandora as messenger" and "Pandora as instrument", but this is probably only one of degree. For, although an instrument can readily "speak" as a messenger, a messenger cannot aspire to perform an instrumental role with equal skill and effect.

From the time it was painted in 1934, Balthus' controversial and rarely seen picture "The Guitar Lesson" has remained a further enigma in his already enigmatic ouevre. Throughout seven decades, art historians and critics have remained baffled by its imagery and the action it appears to represent.

The artist shows a young, possibly pre-pubescent girl, laid out on her music teacher's knee. It is seemingly not for punishment that the girl is so positioned, for she is lying not on her stomach to expose her buttocks for the traditional beating with a hairbrush: she lies instead on her back, with her skirt pulled up to reveal her naked *pubis*. Her teacher is restraining her in this position by grasping a braid of her hair with her right hand, at the same time fingering the inside of the girl's upper left thigh in the area immediately adjacent to her Mound of Venus. As a defensive action, perhaps, the supine girl has torn at the teacher's dress, exposing a diminutive right breast. The guitar – it is not a real, full-size instrument but a small-scale miniature or toy – has been cast aside on the floor prior to the enactment of the ritual Balthus summons us to witness.

It is of little wonder that Nicholas Fox Weber recently asked of this painting[4]: "Who is the victim and who the victimizer?" In the first place we have the question of the "box" itself, which here seems to be represented by the guitar – significantly a toy guitar, a childish thing. As Saint Paul admonished us, the protagonists in the "The Guitar Lesson" have put aside this childish thing to pursue the real stuff life that begins with puberty. The toy guitar is obviously much too small to harness the mature forces of creative power and composition.

This recognition of the inadequacy of a miniature instrument to accommodate an adult (real world) creative (sexual) scenario seems central to our further exploration of "The Guitar Lesson". In a complete inversion of Pandora's "box", the toy guitar of the painting not only presents no threat, it has nothing to offer the protagonists. Its sole function is to provide a clue to the Pandora-role of the girl in the painting. The young girl represents Pandora here, the Pandora we have recognized to be an "instrument". Clearly, Pandora in her youthful and idealized feminine form constitutes a threat to the middle-aged music teacher, who exposes the not yet fully formed instrument (body) of her student with the purpose of demonstrating its shortcomings. The look in the teacher's eyes, however, suggests that she has relaxed her authority, becoming resigned to the fact that her mature experience will be limited now to the oral.

This leads us back to Nicholas Fox Weber's question: "Who is the victim and who the victimizer?" Or does it? What exactly is the "Mystery towards a solution" here? An enigma, certainly, and therefore fitting within the enigmatic genre of Modernism as a whole. A puzzle, of course, but where does it fit within the genre of modern painting? Weber implies that it qualifies as a sado-masochistic gesture, an exercise in the punishment phase of sexual games, which is a somewhat typical interpretation of Balthus's work. Yet "The Guitar Lesson" has so far escaped such a routine assessment. My own suggestion is that the subject matter of this enigmatic work is at once both *classical* and *modern* – a position very close to Balthus's own disclosures about his creative intentions. For example, he repeatedly acknowledges Piero della Francesca as his mentor in painting. Also, "The Guitar Lesson" deals unequivocally with the creative and interpretive processes, while its title suggests that the painting itself is accorded a didactic role in his *oeuvre.*

Although it contains a female form in a state of undress, "The Guitar Lesson" does not really qualify as a nude painting. It might belong rather to the realm of the erotic, except that it lacks the sense of both pain and pleasure, offering only sadness and submission. It may be helpful to recall Piero della Francesca's "Flagellation of Christ", in which the whole cast of historical actors – Pilate, the

[4] *The New Yorker*, 1999

High Priests, those with scourges – that whole cast is in place, all perfectly positioned in an exquisite Early Renaissance architectural frame. The only thing missing is the action: there is no scourging taking place, and Christ is not suffering under the blows of his tormentors. The sado-masochism that haunts so many Italian and Spanish martyrdom paintings of the 16th and 17th centuries is absent.

In much the same way, "The Guitar Lesson" sets the scene and outlines the puzzle, but there is no beating, no torture, no rape, in fact no sexual activity at all. Possibly, the music teacher is playing on the instrument (body) of her favorite pupil, but within the framework of classical mythology this suggests a creative act rather than a teacher sexually violating her sacred charge.

Clearly, this painting distinguishes between the conventional, traditional female nude, that portrays a woman as an object of desire and possession, and a modern treatment of the Pandora-syndrome in which the woman is now revealed as an "instrument" capable of performance and interpretation.

Can we translate this metaphor effectively to the realm of architecture and towards a better understanding of its presence as a box or an instrument? In other words, does its formal configuration simply take the shape of some minimalist container; or does it have a formal expression more like that of a guitar, offering the potential of performance through an instrument that can be strummed, plucked and drummed in pursuit of engaging harmonics and their appropriate variations?

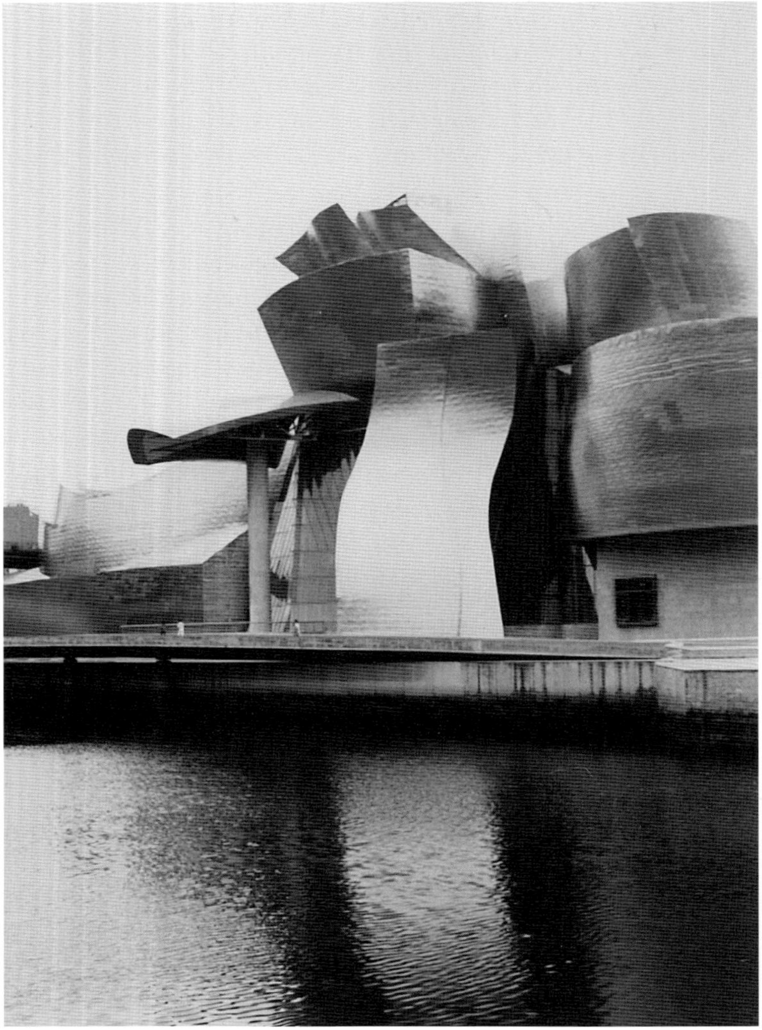

BOX VERSUS INSTRUMENT

Malcolm Quantrill

There have been a wide variety of reactions to work of Canadian-born architect, Frank Gehry, over the past two decades. Naturally, his success is one measure of achievement, but the architecture itself has proved difficult to pidgeon-hole. Of course it is enormous fun, and it is outrageous, too, but where exactly does Gehry fit into the Post-Modern scene? My own examination of his work suggests that the answer is: "Not at all". In fact my conclusion is that Gehry is connected to the mainstream ideas of early Modernism, even Dada, and is indebted most particularly to the pioneering work of Marcel Duchamp and Rene Magritte.

In the early 20th century we still inhabited a world of reality. We will start, therefore, with that reality – at least with Marcel Duchamp's portrayal of reality in 1910, at the beginning of his career as an artist. This portrait of a prostitute is quite unsentimental: her sagging breasts are exaggeratedly large, as are her thighs. But we appreciate the fleshiness of this woman, who has an obviously commercial appeal.

The case of René Magritte's nude is quite different. On the one hand this woman is portrayed in a meticulously realistic style, yet the artist's central idea in *L'evidence eternelle* (Eternal Evidence – as opposed to *L'Evidence Maternelle*, or 'Evidence of Maternity') of 1930 is to dismember and fragment the woman's sexuality. It is as though the desire to possess this ideal woman in her entirety has been thwarted by a process that reveals her to be only available one piece at a time. Thus, the sexual game here resembles stamp collecting, in that possession of all the pieces at any one time seems impossible, and we have to chose between acquiring those perfect breasts, her Mound of Venus or those dimpled knees. And therein lies Magritte's '*Eternal Evidence*', evidence of an Eternal Truth – however hard we may attempt to comprehend the *whole picture* the *whole thing* at a single glance – in reality we can only grasp it one piece at a time.

Magritte shows us the "goddess of sex" as a dismembered woman. By contrast, in Allen Jones' *Table* (1972) the female goddess has been reduced to a servant's position, to a mere supporting role. I want to suggest that this capacity to accommodate such a transformation, this change in roles, may also be applied in demonstrating the *subject / object* condition of architecture. In this way we may distinguish between the objectivity of architecture when it is conceived as a mere "box" – in other words a *thing*, Heidegger's *Das Ding* – a container that "contains" other *things*, – in contrast to its subjectivity when it is designed as a demonstration of a responsive instrument. My proposal is that, conceived and manufactured as a box, architecture has no *persona*, in other words, it cannot be tuned, strummed, brought to life through the medium of performance.

On the other hand, architecture conceived as an "instrument" can be released from the category of a TEXAS inanimate object, to assume through the medium of performance a subjective, and potentially animated form of expression.

2

STEALING A GEM

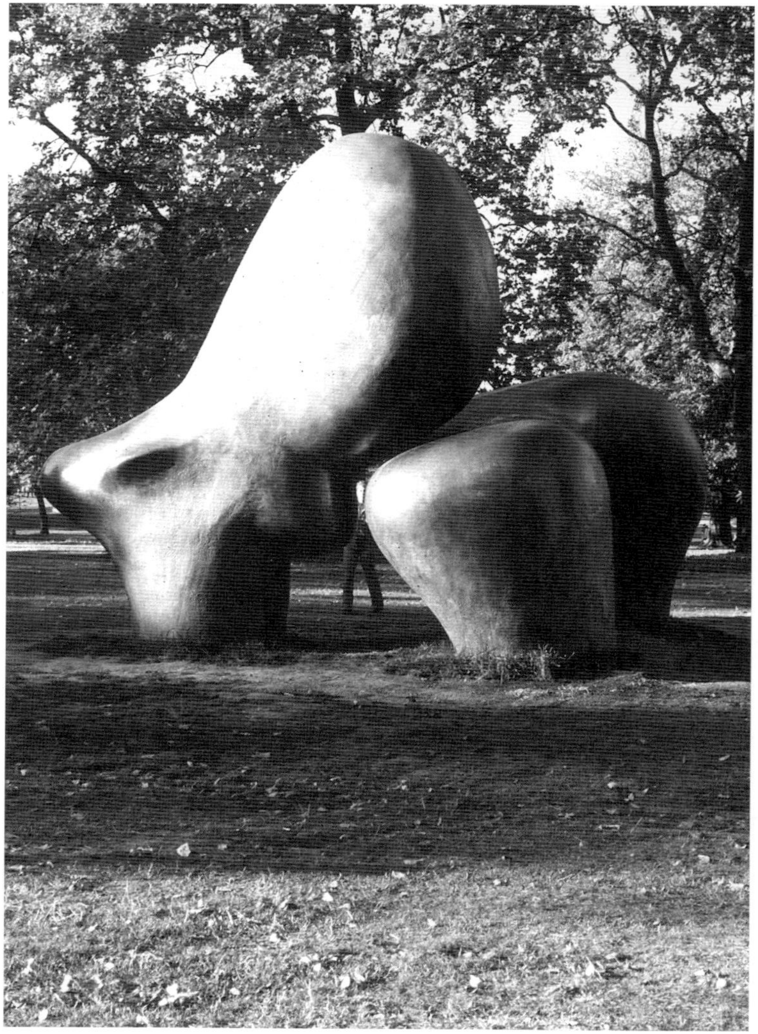

MASTERS OF TWO-PART INVENTIONS

Malcolm Quantrill – Matti K. Mäkinen

MQ: Karsten Harries suggests that "the ethical function of architecture" is to create and to provide an optimum "ethos" for the benefit and enjoyment of humanity. Naturally, we would assume that the environmental expectations for a football field and those for a religious, meditation space should be very different.

MKM: Well, ethics has to do with the correct handling of circumstances, with doing things right. In real life situations, however, we first have to answer the question: "What exactly do we mean by 'right'?"

MQ: Perhaps we should identify an example.

MKM: How about the concept of "sustainable development"? Does that relate to architecture's ethical function? In the late1980s, when we first became aware of its political implications, we soon realized that "sustainability" had its built-in paradoxes. An obvious inconsistency was its apparently easy acceptance by factions that were, in every sense, diametrically opposed to one another.

MQ: It seemed that people of extremely opposite views in the environmental debate were all too eager to step up to the pulpit and preach their version of "sustainable development".

MKM: Precisely, because both its virtues and its vices lay within the variety of interpretations through which it could be applied to programs of practical action.

MQ: "Sustainable development" is commonly thought of in terms of its four main aspects: economic, ecological, social and cultural. Is it then possible for architecture to participate in all those spheres? If so, then architectural ethics could be understood as "behaving correctly", doing the "right thing" in optimizing human benefits within all four spheres of sustainability.

MKM: And that's interesting, because I recall that the Modern Movement in architecture was primarily concerned with just two basic objectives, the political and the social, which together were supposed to add up to our modern culture. Obviously, the inability of our modernist forebears to consider including something approximating to an ecological agenda was a glaring omission.

MQ: But we mustn't forget that the Modern Movement promoted a kind of bare bones architecture. In fact it was rather threadbare, like the working classes it pretended to represent. Although ultimately, of course, the Modern Movement wanted to be seen as intellectual.

MKM: The social card was not played by politicians alone. As a well-known example of our own professional pioneers, we only need to remember the socially tuned statements of the early functionalists. The German architect Bruno Taut wrote in his *Modern Architecture* (1929), that "...the architect becomes creator of an ethical and social character; the people who use the building...will, through the structure of the house, be brought to a better behaviour... Thus architecture becomes the creator of new social observances."

MQ: But we have to remember that modern architecture in the United States lacked these political associations. In America there was a fear of the Left and of a work force organized to break the grip of capitalist commerce and production.

MKM: In this connection, referring to the political dimensions of modern architecture's early phases, we can also remember that architecture was not alone in carrying political messages. Many artists and cultural leaders sang the same songs in their work, faithful to the prevailing ideologies of their time.

MQ: And Le Corbusier stands out as a prime example of this ambition, with his bowler hat, his pipe, his bow-tie, his abstract paintings and his mathematically generated buildings. All these gestures conspire to distance the architect from the workers, the plebeians, whose needs and aspirations he claimed to respond to with his architecture.

MKM: I am not too eager to discuss Corbu. And why not? When I studied in the fifties, he was the holiest prophet among the saints of the modernist faith. In those days we still carried an image of the Paradise of Modernism in our hearts, with the apples hanging untouched in their tree of knowledge of good and evil. In his hey-day, for us and our professors, Corbu was unquestionable, "untouchable" so to say...

MQ: l'Unite d'Habitation was certainly not designed for artisans: it wasn't even designed in response to the French way of life. To isolate the French housewife from her market, to effectively obstruct her pattern of daily shopping for fresh meat and vegetables, was a slap in the face *for La Vie Francaise.*

MKM: Now we have had time enough to fill our stomachs with the apples of knowledge. We have been shaken awake by snakes silently stealing into our paradise, the angriest ones carrying the venom of Post-modernism.

MQ: For Corbu, Modernism offered a new stage on which he could strut and act out his theories. But was his a truly a revolutionary activity, was he a comrade of the workers? For me, he seemed to be replaying the roles of renaissance and neo-classical master architects.

MKM: Of course. Another feature foreign to me is his commonly repeated definition of architecture. You know, while praising functional buildings for practical uses, he tells us that "Architecture is the masterly, correct and magnificent play of masses brought together in light".

MQ: Although Le Corbusier's words may resemble those of a saint, his actions betray him more as a hero. Clearly, he wasn't able to differentiate between them.

MKM: I am fed up with these 'heroes', a struggle for the heroic role which has become altogether too fashionable nowadays. Corbu deserves something better. Just think of the footprints he left on several continents through his own work, and especially the work of his many followers or similarly-minded contemporaries, in India, in Brazil and in Argentina.

MQ: The fact is that from the 1930s to the 1960s, Corbusianism was a kind of a religion: it gave us some sort of *architectural theology.* And as we say of the Curate's egg, "it was not all bad, but good in parts"

MKM: He is a brilliant representative of that generation of architects that gave the air of being capable of urban planning on a scale of millions of inhabitants as well as the detailing down to the scale of door handles and hinges.

MQ: Which seems to bring us back to the question of representation.

MKM: What do you mean? Please explain.

MQ: I mean in the terms of the Message or, in Mc Luhan's terms, *Massage* that Architecture conveys or transmits. We have said here, for example, that Le Corbusier did not respond to the "needs and aspirations of the workers, of the artisans".

MKM: In a way, yes. But before that, let me add that urban plans like that for Chandigarh or, say, Brasilia are incredible monuments – or should I say "rudiments" – of a time where we believed that urban planning on those scales was possible as a one man show. Such incredible, gigantic misinterpretations.

MQ: In what sense? Is it the role of the architect or the role of his architecture that you have in mind?

MKM: Both. Quite definitely both. Maybe what I am shooting down is the belief that architecture in the sense it is mainly understood, as creating order using physical elements, could suffice to solve the multi-disciplinary problems of urban planning. Think of Corbu's definition of architecture as the play of light and shadow; how shallow, naïve and ridiculous it becomes when brought to the level of urbanism.

MQ: Then how does this relate to the notion of "fake"?

MKM: I'm not sure I understand the connection. I believe that Corbu and other masters playing through the whole variety of scales in planning were honest in their intentions. Even Corbu's famous definition I can gladly accept, if I read it as an artist's inspired expression.

MQ: Ethics" just happens to be the first item on the shopping list for this dialogue, while "fake" is the last one.

MKM: In the case of Le Corbusier perhaps we might speak also of misrepresentation? *N'est ce pas?* In ethical terms, what is it that makes for a "true architecture"? Just how does one become a "true architect"? If an architect says: "Look here, I am the real thing, a true architect; and what I do, what I have to offer in this world, is this 'true architecture'", how should we react to that?

MQ: Before we have a chance to judge this man or his creations he tells us what is the case, what he wants us to believe. We might compare such an architect to an advertising agent. One of my design teachers at Liverpool University always referred to Le Corbusier as a "propagandist", saying that his aim was "not to create but rather to indoctrinate".

MKM: And that's true because Corbu proclaims his own assessment of himself and draws his own conclusion that only from such merit can come a perfect work.

MQ: But does not that attitude invalidate both the man and the product? Since we have no choice in the matter of assessing his work, isn't such an architect behaving unethically? Isn't his indoctrination technique merely a means of covering up a certain kind of fake?

MKM: Or could this mean that what we have here is the possibility of conflict between architectural theory and architectural ethics?

MQ: Can we explain how this situation might come into being?

MKM: It probably has to do with the existence of two different scales of values. The one measures how the basic needs of human habitat are fulfilled by the form and fabric of a structure, while the other assesses how that structure, viewed as an "aesthetic object", contributes to human culture.

MQ: So, what we should be looking for here are ways by which those two different scales of values can each achieve optimum satisfaction, avoiding both the temptation to compromise and the generation of conflict between the two?

MKM: In other words, they would achieve a harmonious result by satisfying the programme of physical requirements, while adding an extra, cultural/aesthetic contribution through the unified wholeness of the work.

MQ: Which is precisely what Johan Sebastian Bach managed to create in his Two-Part Inventions. And that might be a helpful way to look at architecture – I mean as a "Two-Part Invention".

MKM: That makes sense, because isn't it true that architects have to satisfy not only the humble household gods, but also those deities of a higher, more sublime order?

MQ: In this context, as architects today seek to enhance their performance and reputation, it would seem both ethical and honourable for them to aspire to be such Masters of Two Part Inventions.

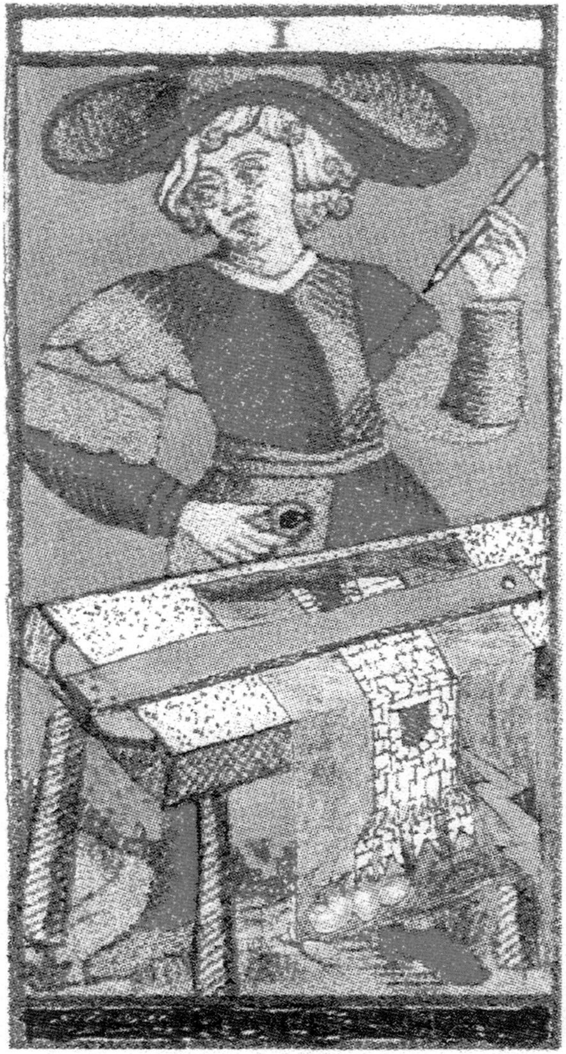
I

DOING THE RIGHT THING

Matti K. Mäkinen

And they were sawing off the branches
on which they were sitting, and eventually
they dropped off and those who watched them
shook their heads and kept on sawing.
Bertolt Brecht

Ethics is about handling things right, doing the right thing. But surely in real life situations, just one question remains. What is right? So, let us try to find some examples.

Could one updated key to open this question be hidden within the concept of "sustainable development"?[1] This political slogan, as it entered our consciousness in the late 1980s, was soon criticised for its built-in paradoxes. One point of criticism focussed on the suspiciously easy acceptance of the idea in very different circles. People representing the most opposite sides of the environmental interests and conflicts were too easily ready to step to the pulpit in the robes of defenders and promoters of sustainable development – whatever that might mean. The main explanation may be found in the freedom left for interpretations, in turning the concept into practical actions.

Sustainable development is commonly interpreted as consisting of four principal elements: economic, ecological, social and cultural development. Let us suppose that architecture would have a substantial share in all of these playgrounds. Then the ethics of architecture could be analysed through the idea of doing the right things from the economic, ecological, social and cultural points of view.

To illustrate this subdivision, keeping architecture as my point of departure, I'll take some examples.

[1] There is no general agreement on exactly what sustainable development means. This lack of clarity is not without its advantages. It has, for example, allowed groups with different and often conflicting interests to reach some common ground upon which concrete policies have been developed. See Susan Baker (ed.), The Politics of Sustainable Development. Theory, Policy and Practice Within the European Union, Routledge, London, 1997.

Firstly, economy. Man builds in order to satisfy a need. Can someone's greed be a need? One thing seems sure, ecologically, socially and culturally motivated needs can also be economically justified and right.

Secondly, ecology. Doing the right things within the field of ecology is not necessarily so easily explored. It leads to further questions about man's position within the global ecology. Of these four elements of sustainable development, ecology is the one most closely related to original nature and the local culture. The other three elements, while strongly culture-bound, accentuate the "development" factor, man the developer.

Thirdly, social aspects. What do they include? At least the questions of sustainable society, the problems of finding the right solutions from the point of view of communities, society and mankind as a great family. Also, the problems of equality and welfare in whatever ways the well-being of different kinds of people living in different places and conditions can be affected by architecture.

And finally the fourth factor: culture. Culture is the "custom of the house". Isn't custom our second nature, according to the formulation of Blaise Pascal? A culture is a system of standard situations, as Christopher Alexander has defined it. Alfred W. Crosby, professor of history, speaks of certain modes of behaviour, and about how man's ability to keep these alive over generations constitutes what we call culture.[2]

Our attitudes towards the other three elements of sustainable development are controlled, even dictated by this fourth element, our cultural climate. Culture is the ultimate judge when we try to find a balance between right and wrong. But this leads, in turn, to one further question. And that is the relation between culture and change, culture and progress, culture and time. To what extent should we allow change in our house customs, our standard situations, shattered by the wheel of time rolling on?

And, this said, back to architecture. On the one hand, architecture stands for the durable, the long-lived, the history of nations, the memory of mankind. On the other, architecture has "always" been characterized by repeatedly changing modes, styles, even fashions. The prevailing *zeitgeist* has dictated whether to oppose the pressures and keep to the old or to rush ahead of the actual present to be the first to catch the news.

In David Watkin's view: "architecture is an art with its own traditions, and not a science, so that its concern with image-making is no less vital than its solution of practical problems".[3] Interpreting some of Viollet-le-Duc's texts, Watkin points to him as "one of those writers who see only two possible

[2] See A. W. Crosby, Ecological Imperialism, Cambridge University Press, Cambridge, 1986.
[3] David Watkin, Morality and Architecture, Oxford University Press, Oxford, 1977.

alternatives for architecture: either as capricious fashion, arbitrary and trivial, or as the expression of some external centre of gravity, such as social and political ideals, technological necessity, or the spirit of the age. For those who adhere to this outlook, the existence of an artistic tradition with its own canons of judgement and its own standards does not occur."

Although Viollet-le Duc wrote his *Discourses* in the late 19th century, a good part of the above interpretations still retain their validity. Capricious trickery as one of the favoured roads to fame is still an object of both flattery and criticism. Technological necessities have been brought to daylight, on the one hand, as expressions of progress and subtle inventiveness and, on the other, they exist as theatrical image building and an over-emphasis of "mock-engineering".

The political messages of architecture are well known, especially as consciously used by the superpowers of the 20th century. Socially tuned propaganda goes hand in hand with the political one. But the social card was not played by politicians alone. As a well known example of our own professional pioneers, we only need to remember the socially tuned phrases of the early functionalists. The German architect Bruno Taut wrote in his "Modern Architecture" (1929) of how "...the architect becomes creator of an ethical and social character; the people who use the building...will, through the structure of the house, be brought to a better behaviour... Thus architecture becomes the creator of new social observances." In this connection, referring to the political dimensions of the early phases of modern architecture, we can also remember that architecture was not alone in carrying political messages. Many artists and cultural personalities sang the same tunes through their work, faithful to the leading ideologies of their time.

And now, updating the "zeitgeist", the language of architecture today can be read and easily understood all over the world. It says: "money". Money is the leading force, money is the ultimate symbol illuminating the entire web of market ideology, a web woven in layered and criss-crossing patterns all around our lives and culture. In the spirit of the time, as seen in the world of architecture, the invisible hands of swiftly operating capital are holding the controls. How far this is intentional, and how far just a by-product of a rush after higher esteemed values than architecture, we can only wonder.

One thing seems certain. Repeatedly we meet evidence of peoples' search for images of domesticity, something to identify themselves with. And failing to produce this has been seen as one of the most fatal sins of modern architecture. A curious feature can be traced upon a closer look at this search for home. It has to do with our basic nostalgias. Maybe we instinctively see that a genuine home is not so easily found or built at the present time. Then our search tends to be directed either backwards in time, animated by an idea of returning to a former epoch. Or others turn their eyes towards a better future, in order to build a home unlike any existing one, better than the one they once left. The former group follow their nostalgias, the latter their utopias. But who votes for a house in the present?

The ethos in architecture is not only functional; you will – and have to – find its ethos in the structural qualities and in the realm of meanings. Meanings submitted, meanings read and interpreted, meanings that are *lived.*

Some other examples of "independently operated rules" – I don't believe in a common network of "ethical guidelines" – might include the following, to mention only some points that come to mind. Looking for some degree of order, I have adopted here the tripartite subdivision of functions, structures and meanings.

Functions: As to the functional side, I only want to add – repeating Umberto Eco's view – that submitting meaning is also a function.

Structures: One traditional rule is that the structural frame be sound. This means durability, but even sparing and economical solutions have a functioning relation to the uses of the building as well as to the supplementary parts of its construction. That also means an ecological, economic and even cultural understanding in choosing the materials and forms. Here, after enumerating some – at least to some extent – measurable qualities, we end up with culture. Here, we enter the realm of immaterial – and even immeasurable – structures and we are ready to pass over to meanings.

Meanings: The meanings connected with a work of architecture can have links to history and *Zeitgeist*, presently prevailing or past. The meanings are born not only out of the looks and the common atmosphere around the building, they also pop up through narratives, stories told and beliefs held, not to speak of the hardware of knowledge. The sources of meanings are the circumstances and the organisations, public or private, or the persons who gave birth to the building. The intentions of all of these add their ethical values to the work. From our point of view, the ideas, aims and intentions of the responsible architect earn their special interest. But, finally, the meaning is not contained in the building, but rather it is in "the eye of the beholder".

And what about the good, the beautiful, and the right? How do we interpret these concepts and turn them into practical action? In what Roger Connah terms "archi-babble", there is so much talk about the 'good environment'. And the troubles begin when you start analysing. The first thing you bump into is the multi-faceted quality of the "environment". You look around and see that you are surrounded by not only physical environment – be it architecture or not – but also simultaneously you have to count with economic, political, social, cultural environments – whatever they happen to be. For the time being, you find yourself also wrapped within the layers of invisible webs and many of the environmental concepts are re-organised or interpreted as networks.

What, then, is a good environment? Or a beautiful landscape? What is welfare, well-being, the good life? And speaking of welfare, I would start to Iook for an answer in the real sense, not in terms of Gross National Product or the various other indicators of growth.

These questions invite further questioning. For example: A good environment for whom? The young? The elderly? The poor, the rich, the healthy and the active? Or the handicapped with their crutches? The happy ones, the sad, the disappointed and the angry?

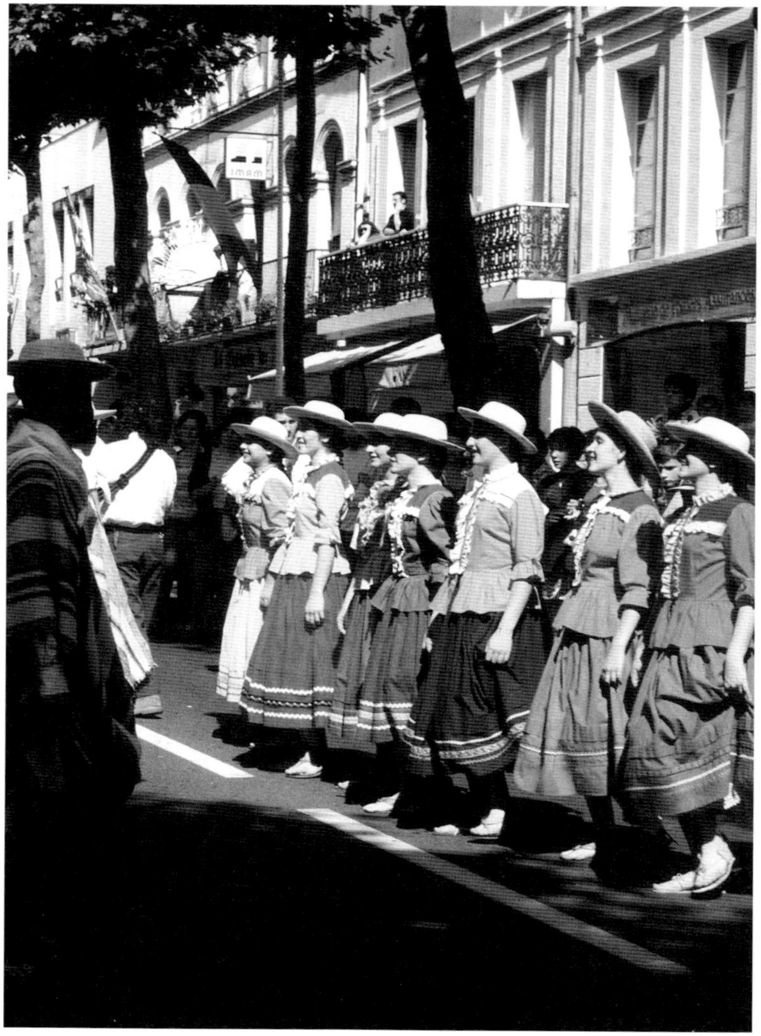

MASTER BUILDERS OR PUPPETS ON A STRING?

Matti K. Mäkinen

When I was studying architecture, some half a century ago, I felt ashamed and nearly panicked when I realized that I had been studying architecture for three years and still hadn't caught the idea of what it is all about. If I have some ominous feelings concerning the concept of architecture it's because I still don't know, what it *is*.

Then my eyes opened: how could I know what it is, when not a single one of our distinguished professors of architecture had told us? Maybe it was connected to some secret *regalia* kept in the vaults of the profession's high priests?

I was too shy to stand up and ask, especially as I thought that all the others knew the answer. So I went on studying, playing as nonchalant and omnipotent as all my fellow students. Yet, in my secret folders, I started collecting definitions of architecture. I had a collection of nearly 300 answers to my mute questions, when one day I simply lost the papers and since then I have been compelled to wander through professional life without this valuable aid. One thing I realised: that nearly all the heroes who had become Names on the map of architecture had seen it as their right and duty to make a statement on the theme. But not our professors – they passed by the definitions, they just went on teaching the know-how. Later on, I became a professor myself and then I was better prepared to understand the why's and why not's.[1]

One thing I learned. I asked myself, what if one of my students stands up after my lecture and asks the crucial question? What shall I say? That I, a professor of architecture, really don't know? With this horrid vision in mind, I explored my soul and decided, that if necessary, I'll firmly use the words I heard from the Finnish architect and professor Keijo Petäjä: "Architecture is a built state of mind".

As simple as that! The best is that with a second thought you see how the path of thought forks out. The state of mind…reflected in the form of a building…Is it the state of mind of the architect

[1]Aulis Blomstedt, architect and professor, once asked his students: "What is architecture?". The students glanced at one another, none of them willing to answer. After a moment's silence, Blomstedt continued: "Don't be too concerned, I don't know either."

completing his act of creation? Or is it the collective mentality of the time, the *zeitgeist,* and of all the people sharing this spirit of the time?

Architects of my age were educated to profess to the spirit of modernism, the last and final end station of a long succession of 'isms'. It took a few decades, before doubt eroded our sincere faith, as Vincent Scully reports:[2]

"From that dream we've awakened, and those of us from my generation who were deeply marinated in modernism can hardly believe what has happened to us. Today most of us can hardly remember some of the things we believed as gospel thirty years ago."

Northrup Frye, a former professor of literature says that "It is impossible to teach or learn literature, what one teaches and learns is criticism".[3] Translated to the language of architecture: you cannot teach or learn architecture, what you teach or learn is criticism.

Architectural criticism is a very delicate matter. The closest relative to architecture is context. The context where architecture is delivered, where it lives, ages and eventually even dies. Criticism is one focal context. The theory of criticism is the theory of architecture.

Wayne Attoe has made a list of the different types of architectural criticism:[4]

– Normative criticism is mainly exercised by the different bodies of bureaucracy, high-ranking authorities or teachers. Their assesments are made with reference to established norms, laws, regulations, standards or recommendations derived from authorities, organisations or research institutes.

– Interpretative criticism is exercised in order to influence. One form is the advocatory branch of criticism, representing and marketing the views of a certain group in the name of shared interest or ideology. Even the teaching of architecture is all but value-free…just go and listen what they say!

– Descriptive criticism depicts the object or the history of how it came about. It can tell stories of the key persons of a project, or the backgrounds of the undertaking. The object or subject can be the author, the architect , even his family, his home or his office, including other key persons. Even biographies are a popular type of this descriptive form of architectural criticism.

– Contextual criticism is an important branch of the descriptive approach. Architecture understood as a "text in a context" has been named "contextual architecture", which in several discourses is interpreted as a piece of architecture fitting into its (physical) place or its time in the course of history. Very often the main attention is then given to the object's appearance, its period, its style,

[2] Vincent Scully: "Urban Architecture Awakens from a Bad Dream", Urbanities, Vol. 4, 1994

[3] Northrup Frye: The Stubborn Structure, Cornell University Press, Ithaca, 1970

[4] Wayne Attoe: *Architecture and Critical Imagination*, Sutton, Surrey, 1978

its more or less harmonious relation to a wider townscape or landscape. In some writings the other contexts, like those of social, cultural or economic conditions are considered.

Architecture is mainly interpreted as a product of an architect, with the exception of the nameless builders of *architettura minore*, vernacular building, in which resulting structures have not necessarily reached the sophisticated level of *Baukunst*, of *architecture*. Every work of art is unique, just as an individual is unique, and the work's singularity is indebted to the artist's unique personality. Society certainly takes part in forming that personality, but the creative act is her or his own, not of the class of which the artist happened to be a member. Even in collective efforts, like quilting and manufacturing processes, a series of decisions are the result of individual contributions.[5]

Even an artist-oriented architect is seldom the only creator of a building. Another important, often powerful, creator is the context; and – to widen the vistas of contextuality in architecture – we can leave the building standing in its time and place and direct our attention instead to the innumerable links in the chain of causalities that affect the work at all stages of a construction process.

At the start of the design, the architect needs a commission – a client. The client needs to recognise a need. The client needs resources to hire the architect. He needs money for both the design and the implementation. He needs a programme to analyse his needs. He may also need investors. The architect needs his own skill, his staff and the office facilities. It's not necessary here to make a list of the needs of the numerous parties engaged during the construction phases of our piece of architecture. Two crucial resources have to be mentioned: the architect needs a suitable reputation to get the commission, and then he needs a strong character to carry it through to a happy conclusion. And last but not least, if his intentions really are to deliver a piece of architecture, he must be a combination of a fearless hero on the everyday battlefields of construction work and a smiling, utterly flexible negotiator at moments of darkening skies and crisis lurking around the next corner.

When the work is completed and the building stands there, the architect may get the opportunity to read his name on the pages of professional magazines. In those stories, there is mainly one hero, the Master builder, i.e. the Architect. But in many cases the name of the game is: Who was the architect, the designated Architect or the Context in which more than 90% of the real decisions were made? In other words: Who played the pipe, who spanned the string, and who was the puppet to dance on it?

[5] T. Kaori Kitao, from the Internet <http://www.swarthmore.edu/Humanities/tkitao1/artHist.html> (06.01.2000).

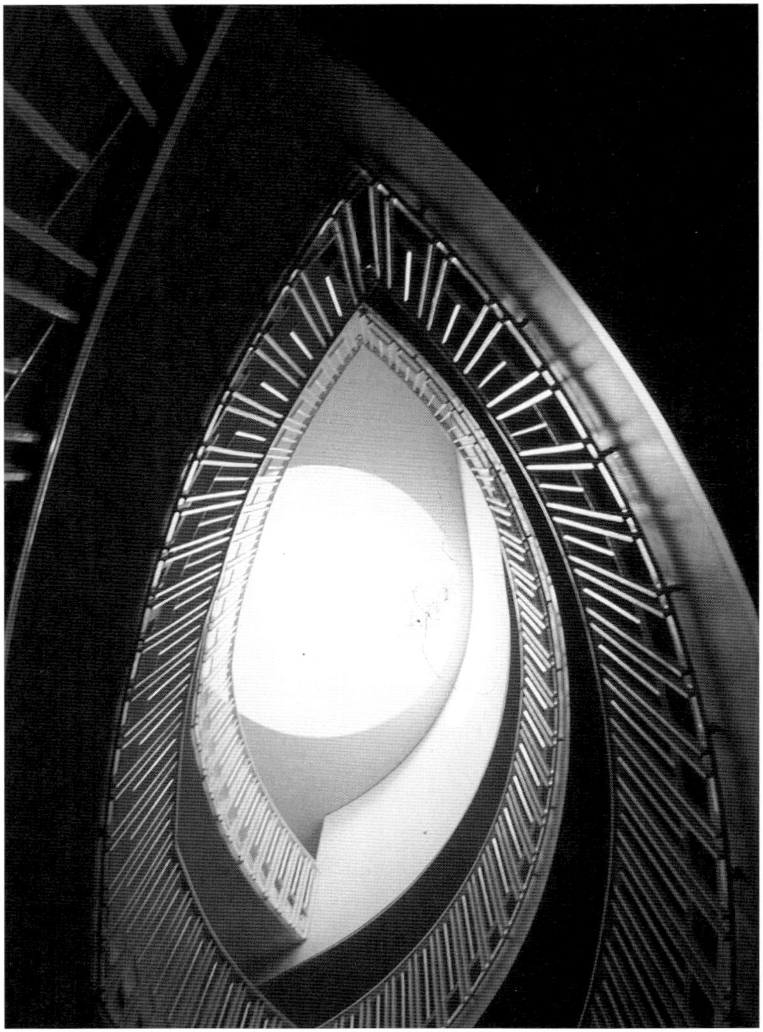

THE ART OF STEALING A GEM

Matti K. Mäkinen

What is this *thing* called Architecture?

Sometimes it looks like this was the most essential and most important question concerning this Thing. So much has been written, so much belief and disbelief has been attached to this concept – and to attempts to find out, understand, interpret and explain it.

In an earlier letter, my friend Malcolm writes of "Sister Architecture". This is the first time I have the possibility of meeting this sister in so familiar circumstances. I have been used to seeing architecture as a mother, the Mother of all Arts, one step more distanced than a sister. It has been easy to imagine this mother gathering all the other arts around herself, offering shelter for music as well as literature, providing a background for sculpture and painting. When I study this mother's face on, say, the façade of Ihne's Staatsbibliotek in Berlin, I have the mother smiling at me with her stern Prussian countenance, but simultaneuously the children gathered around, the decorations all over softening the scenery. Behind, in the clouds, I also see the *gestalt* of the grandfather, architect of the Imperial Court Ernst von Ihne with his sword and uniform, a misty ghost from times past. And, having read in my books of the corrupted years of Historicism, I can smell the rusty iron and the brutal concrete hidden behind Ihnes' crumbling décor.

Another picture pops up here. The first time I saw Mies van der Rohe's Seagram Building in New York. I stood on the street one morning in the spring of 1960. I stood there, staring and I thought: What a gem. So pure and so distinctly different from the old, maybe nineteenth century highrises that framed its setting. The fine proportioning of the mullions, the clear-cut contours of the mass told their story of typical Miesian precision. Revisiting the place 20 years later I had to realise that the gem was stolen, the dream had faded. A close study of the environment was necessary before I understood that the gem was still there, but the context, the historical masquerade, had been replaced by modern highrise buildings. What had once been a pioneering feat had lost its glory. This is not the only case where it is difficult to estimate the extent to which the architecture dwells in the building and how much is due to the context. But a grim irony seems also to exist in this Seagram case, where the sparkle of the original gem has been dimmed by its surroundings, by the existence of more mediocre buildings of steel and glass, of awkward towers that give only faint evidence of the Miesian tradition. You come close to Baudrillard's theorizing about the original and the *simulachra.*

Who am I to analyse the wonders of New York? I'm just another visitor from across the ocean. Still, I cannot help feeling supported by a writing in which Vincent Scully[1] studies the changing scenery of the Big Apple. He writes of "the martyrology of preservation", and names Penn Station as the first great Martyr. He moves towards Park Avenue and Grand Central, and gives an edgy example of architectural criticism:

"Out of that loss came the ordinance of 1965, so that New York City had the power, moving into the early Seventies, to save the great waiting room in Grand Central Station. However, it was too late to save that wonderful free space of Park Avenue, with its beautiful running of the traffic around Grand Central's office tower. It was too late to save that from the PanAm Building, which was sited the wrong way, should have been turned in the other direction, and is primitively detailed in a manner that's very difficult for us to really understand now."

Scully goes on up north on Park Avenue, continuing his excursion and states: "We began to learn that there were difficulties in defining urban volumes with glass. We began to learn that it wasn't only a question of saving buildings, but of saving the urban environment as a whole. We began to see that the streets were themselves buildings, and had to be thought of in that way. We learned back in 1967 that it was the relationship of buildings to each other to make an urban place that counted as a principle: we later came to call contextuality."

And still further up north, at the level of Central Park, Scully touches the untouchable: "Even when one looks at a more genial building like the Guggenheim, one realizes that it depends on the civility of the buildings around it. Though Wright constantly said that we should think of the museum as being in the park rather than on the street, he is nevertheless exploiting the civility of the other buildings along the street. If those buildings were torn down and everybody put Guggenheims there, the street would become a strip."

This excursion with Vincent Scully leads us further into the very many-faceted problematic of Buildings in Context, and adds to our catalogue of stolen gems. We come to the question of whether

[1] Vincent Scully, , "Urban Architecture Awakens from a Bad Dream", *Urbanities*, Autumn 1994, Vol. 4.

architecture is bound to be a relative rather than an absolute concept. And whether the mainstreams of sustainable architecture are routed in or out of the city-centres.

In Finland, our most typical context for modern architecture has been a non-urban environment, often a location that remains in close contact with nature. This leads us to a very real challenge of creating a model for contemporary Finnish urban planning. And leaving ways open for architecture to enter the city.

One of the things to be observed when studying the family portrait of Architecture is the vague relationship between the different scales of architecture. How about Uncle Town-planning. What is his relation to the other members of the family? To make it clear: is the planning of a town still architecture? Was it ever? In the early times of the ancient Roman military camps? Karlsruhe? Or Chandigarh? Could it be, can it be?

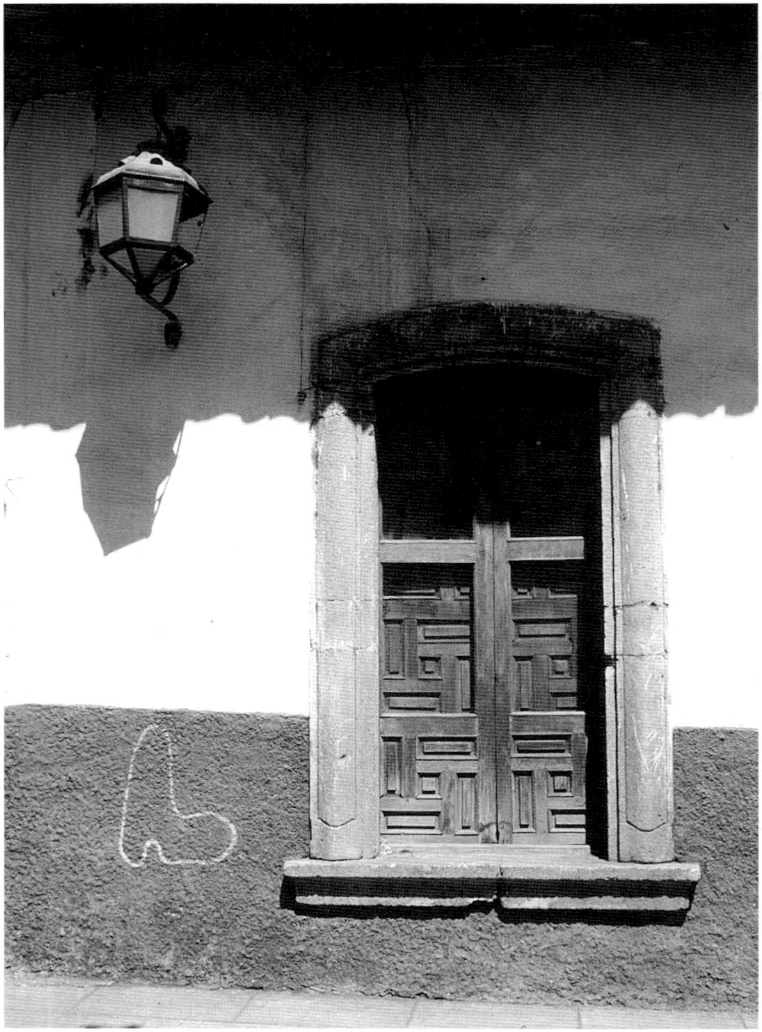

LOS QUENTOS DEL HOGAR FIRESIDE CHATS

Malcolm Quantrill

In the early 1920s, a group of young Finnish architects, led by Hilding Ekelund, went to Italy to study the anonymous architecture of Tuscany and Umbria. This kind of building is known in Italian as *architettura minore* – literally "lesser architecture". It was the time when Finland was just beginning to emerge as an independent nation, and those young Finns were in search of appropriate sources for the next generation of Finnish architecture – one that could be free of the Romantic Classic style that had become the dominant influence in all Scandinavian architecture after the First World War. Although they did not succeed in converting native Italian sources into new, style-free forms for Finnish architecture, what they saw and recorded has remained significant. As recently as 1984 a study of the anonymous farmhouse architecture of Tuscany, published as *La Casa Colonica in Toscana*, focused once again on the terrain that attracted Ekelund and his colleagues 80 years earlier.

Most of us have the privilege of knowing about houses because we have been born and brought up in one. For those of us, therefore, *la casa* is both a "first home" and a "second womb": a house has sheltered us in our initial and most vulnerable period of existence. Those who are not so privileged, those without "a house to call home" – refugees, for example – commonly begin their lives in some hotel room, a railway carriage, or even a roadside barn. For the outcasts of our societies, those who know no *Gemeinschaft*, have literally been thrown out of the house, banished from the privileged life of domesticity to become "homeless".

La casa or *la vivienda* is, for most of us, the source of all formal and spatial concepts. Because most of us are conceived in a house, and because our roots in the "house-womb" are fertilized by our early encounters with the *chiaroscuro* of its light and shapes, the conceptual framework of *la casa* becomes the mould for our future grasp of *being in the world*. The experience we gather from the house that is "our home" therefore helps build our invention of new shapes and spaces. As I have suggested before, what we commonly call "intuition" is nothing more than the unconscious recall of previously acquired knowledge that is then reapplied outside its original context[1].

We have probably also experienced *la casa* as the "stage" for family life, because the house sets the scenes for community and love and more fervent expressions of passion. Perhaps we are better protected from assaults on the house as "shelter" at the movies, when we witness violence as an external force, a condition to be observed but not experienced. Love is a necessary element in our bonding with the house. As its walls are held together by cement, its various rooms and hallways are gathered into a *recitative* through our affectionate memories of the times we have spent in them. This bonding of men and women to the forms and spaces of their surroundings constitutes an essential component of what I have called *The Environmental Memory* (New York, 1987).

Love for *la casa* is like some invisible glue that fixes us in a unique relationship to the house as home. We cannot escape the adhesive power of this compound. Empty rooms, too, those spaces we have long since abandoned, can still exercise an elastic grasp on our psyche. Even those who have never read Gaston Bachelard's *Poetics of Space* will find themselves travelling in their minds through spaces of one or another of the houses they have inhabited, recalling geometric explorations to which their sensibilities have become permanently attached. *La casa* is a repository of our hopes and dreams, it holds bright echoes of our spirit within its coves and cornices long after these have faded from sight: it is a poetic being, whose spiritual domain cannot be entered until we pass through her tangible *epidermis,* and seek her vital, subcutaneous rhythms.

A small book on house design, written by three American architects was published in the early 1970s. Two of the authors, Charles Moore and Donlyn Lyndon are celebrated for their innovative West Coast residential development known as 'Sea Ranch'. The book is called *The Place of Houses* and the authors' intention was to generate a popular movement for achieving a higher standard in the design and making of private houses. They confessed that they had originally set out to produce a new pattern book for individual residences, an ambition inspired by those nineteenth century pattern books describing a variety of houses that people could copy or use as models in realizing their own dwellings. Their assumption was based on their view that "houses built today are mostly constructed without due care", while in the Victorian period they had been well built. They asked themselves whether it was the patterns that had been mostly responsible for this higher standard, and they decided "No": the most important ingredient in making houses is the "care and concern" with which they are put together, because it is this attention to detail "that gives shape to our lives".

[1] *Ritual and Response in Architecture*, London, 1974

This suggested to the authors that no new pattern book, however ingenious and detailed in content, would make any noticeable impact on private house design and execution. In the light of this finding, they initially placed emphasis on the following aspects of contemporary house-making:
(1) That the role of "good taste" in house design be replaced by reference to "tradition";
(2) That the art of house-making should not be seen as an educated or tutored skill, but as one that may be practiced by "anyone who *really cares to create a house of "great worth";* by binding together the essential trappings of one's life together with one's dreams;
(3) That the role of professional expertise in the process should not be minimized, only that professional mystification should be discredited;
(4) Demystification seems to equate here with making such expertise more readily and generally available, which translates into the act of sharing professional knowledge with the client.

The concept of "shelter", a roof over one's head, a house of one sort or another, has played a prominent part in the evolution of Western civilization, especially from the early days of Christianity and the institutionalization of the Church within the Roman Empire. We might recall that there was no shelter available, not even "room at the inn", when the Christ-Child was born in Bethlehem. Indeed, Christ is a permanent icon for the homeless of this world, and he is characterized in Handel's *Messiah*, as being "despised and rejected".

The House of Life envelopes us and shapes our *being*, creating both inner privacy and outward prospects. It does this by balancing the sometimes conflicting demands for opacity and transparency, for formality and intimacy, creating a kaleidoscope of restful shade and energizing sunlight. In the House of Life both walls and roofs may play different roles in enclosing and shading, in establishing and shaping living spaces. It is in the ordering of interior arrangements, and their relation to such exterior spaces and functions as are moulded by courtyards, patios, terraces and gardens, that the House of Life weaves a complex fabric from shifting patterns of contrasting forms and hues.

The inadequacies of a tawdry developer's house are soon spotted by this lack of complexity, for what at first sight may appear to be complex is nothing more than a few cheap tricks designed to deceive the uneducated eye. In such houses of poor substance the formal gestures are weak to sloppy, completely lacking in a value for geometry, entirely devoid of respect for materials or any understanding of their details.

Although Piero della Francesca's painting of *La Nativita* shows a semblance of protecting roofing over the Holy Family, there are a number of holes in the fabric, pieces are actually missing! The sheltering quality of a roof is therefore denied. This lack of security against the elements foreshadows the sentencing of Christ to death. Indeed, it serves as a continual reminder that what we call the "death sentence" is the ultimate denial of shelter to a fellow human being, the irremedial destruction of our roof in this world, the final denial of even the most fragile shelter. Those who are sentenced to die are put out of "house of life" and shut in the "death house".

The authors of *The Place of Houses* want us to believe that "the art of making houses is not an educated skill". But how then do we gain knowledge of traditions, about cultural forms and values? Is this where architectural theory comes in handy? Is the example of such master architects as Adolf Loos and Le Corbusier helpful to us in this house-making process?

In her essay 'The Split Wall: Domestic Voyeurism', Beatriz Colomina cites a fragment from Le Corbusier's *Urbanisme* (1925): "Loos told me one day (that) ... a cultivated man does not stare out of his window; his window is made of ground glass; its purpose is to allow light in not to let the gaze pass out."

She points out that, in Loos houses, the furniture is frequently arranged so that one has to sit with one's back to a window, conducting one's view through the interior of the house rather than out from it. Another Loos detail requires one to look back to the lobby through which one has just entered, reviewing the interior spaces in a logical progression forward. And Colomina continues: "... there is a raised seating area off the living room with a sofa set against the window. One cannot see out of that window but its presence is strongly felt. Bookshelves surrounding the sofa, plus the natural light coming from behind, suggest a comfortable reading nook. But the comfort in this space is not merely sensual, it is also psychological. The position of the couch implies security. Anyone ascending the stairs from the entrance and entering the living room would not immediately be aware of somebody seated on the sofa. By the same token, a person seated in that area would detect the intrusion of another at once, just as an actor coming on stage is immediately seen by spectators in a theatre box..."

Colomina links the windows that seem inevitably behind one in the Loos interior with the views she identifies from the secret "boxes" that look down on the domestic theatre of the social structure which he defined as house. But she fails to reference an important Oriental model for such domestic arrangements; and that model, carried across Europe by the Turks, is the concept of the Islamic house.

The Arab house is centred on privacy. The entry or "public area" is usually quite small and completely cut off from the rest of the house. This entry area is essentially the domain of the men of the house, while the rest of the family practices a sequestered way of life in which only family members have access to its privileges and rituals. Christopher Alexander has pointed out that the traditional house in many cultures shares a spatially interpreted social structure which he defined as a "privacy gradient".

Alexander's research was actually carried out in the residential patterns of Peruvian society. His "privacy gradient" describes the ordering of spaces spanning from the point of entry into the house (where the public "outer" world meets the inner world of family privacy) to the innermost sanctum of family life, the parents' bedroom. In the Arab/Muslim world, no woman is permitted to be seen in the public/reception area, nor may they be seen from such a public area; while the parents' bedroom – the hub of sexual life and recreation – is reserved exclusively for the dalliance and pleasure of the parents.

Alexander's *privacy gradient* has two essential components:
(1) "the exclusivity of physical space"; and
(2) "the exclusivity of visual access".

The Arab/Muslim house is frequently centred on a courtyard, which corresponds to the *atrium* of the Roman villa or the Christian monastic *claustrum* (Latin: locked, barred or enclosed space) "cloister" and acts as a shaded and protected fulcrum for the privacy of family or community life. It is around such a courtyard that a congregation of rooms effectively obstructs any possibility of "transparency": the views from any one room to another are blocked or screened by the manipulation of walls or the plan arrangement.

At a much larger scale, we can see this intimate world reconstructed in the Alhambra at Granada, Spain. In the Arab house there is the further requirement that women be made virtually invisible: not only must they be kept out from sight of strangers within the walls of the house, they must also be screened from gaze of strangers who happen to pass by in the street. To accommodate this latter stricture, Arab craftsmen invented and perfected exquisite wooden grilles, called *mishrabia.* These exquisite elements, which take the form of window panels, or better still become projecting bay windows, allow the women of the household to look out over the terrain below while remaining hidden and anonymous.

Viennese culture received and adapted a number of traces from Oriental thought and practice, and the curiosities and anomalies of Loos' domestic *Raumplannung* provide further evidence of this influence. For instance, the ground glass window pane, that admits light but obstructs a view of the outside world, seems to be nothing more than an inversion of the *mishrabia* principle. From such a vantage point, perched above the main level of circulation, the ladies could survey the male-dominated interior of the house. It was as though they enjoyed all the advantages of a female divan, benefiting from a reversal of power, which endowed them with an inverted authority over the orders of space stretched out below them.

The function and effect of the so-called "picture window" offer a complete contrast. Although Le Corbusier was probably not its inventor, he almost certainly patented it, and Colomina enthusiastically supports this view. She confirms that Le Corbusier's houses contain the very reverse of the Loos interior. Photographs reveal that his windows are never covered by curtains and their prospects are always directed towards the exterior, suggesting that these houses be read as frames for views of the outside. Even when one is in an exterior space, on a terrace or a *toit-jardin*, walls are positioned to frame the landscape.

But we know that Le Corbusier was not interested in "gardens" or "the landscape" *per se*. As with another "bowler-hatted artist", Rene Magritte, Le Corbusier's "love of nature" sought out rather the terrain of the female nude, the varied landscape of a woman's body: from the *Wanderlust* of her breasts to the languishing valleys of her thighs. In stark contrast to our experience of the Loos house, Colomina affirms, our perception in a Corbusier house "occurs in motion", so that we are removed from the static, Classical world and projected into "a dynamic realm of energy, of movement in space". In contrast to the "still-life" landscape of the rural countryside, the landscape of a woman's body ultimately belongs to animation, as proof of which Corbusier's "picture windows" frame such *landscapes* as Matisse's *La Danse* (1909).

Let us return to the notion of *The Place of Houses*, to the question of where the house belongs in our lives and in our consciousness. Do we perceive our relationship to the house as a static one, in which that house is a fixed and essentially unchanging *object*, to which we conform as though in some ritual with the purpose of placating its Household Gods? That surely describes the condition of the Classical house and its Renaissance and Neo-Classical successors, and it is that condition which determines our experience on visiting a Palladian villa.

Walter Benjamin, in his essay 'Experience and Poverty', describes the messy and thoughtless attack upon the owner's culture that is revealed on entering a bourgeois German residence of the 1880s: the strongest impression one gets from its comfortable and peaceful affluence is that "there is nothing to look for" – because there is no place where the dweller has not already left his traces: knickknacks on the shelves, a cover on the armchair, a screen in front of the fireplace: all leave their traces.

Benjamin recalls a line from a poem by Berthold Brecht, which says: "Cover your tracks", and comments that in the bourgeois home the very opposite attitude prevails: "Moreover, the *interieur* forces the inhabitant to adopt the greatest possible number of habits, habits that correspond more to that *interieur* than to himself".

In *Architecture and Thought* (New York, 1990) Francesco dal Co comments on Benjamin's observations:

"This particularization of every interior is at once both an impoverishment and an attempt to overcome it. For every dwelling denies its own existence as a place when, once inhabited, it becomes marked by the traces of habits that negate or mask its essential character."

And he continues by remarking on Nietzsche's conclusion that: ..."the most characteristic feature of this modern man lies in the strange contrast of (having) an interior to which there is no corresponding exterior, and an exterior to which there is no corresponding interior, (and that) the whole of modern culture is essentially internal."

What effect then does the modern house have on our lives? Within the realms of the glass box and the open plan, how much privacy can the modern house offer us? What sense of intimacy can we expect from a glass pavilion modelled on the display window of a department store? How have modern architects treated opacity and transparency, represented in Gottfried Semper's differentiation of *die Mauer* (a wall of substance) and *die Wand* (a mere screen)?

While I was teaching at Louisiana State University in Baton Rouge during the late1950s, I met a Greek architect, Eustace Papavas by name, whose practice in the State Capital consisted mainly of designing crisply modern houses for young faculty members. Those houses were good looking and his clients enjoyed living in them. But beneath the surface of their contentment lurked an unanticipated threat, for it is written in the Laws of Progress that, if young faculty want to seek promotion and prosperity they should be prepared to move to another university and another house. Unfortunately, those upwardly mobile young families soon discovered that the value they assigned to the enjoyment of their Papavas houses did not have a correspondingly high value in the minds of prospective buyers.

Papavas received a number of adverse comments about his Baton Rouge houses, including: "There's no character here. Where is that old Louisiana charm?" and "Louisiana is famous for its building style, for those grand plantation mansions and the Old Quarter in New Orleans. But here we are in Louisiana and there ain't no Louisiana here!" Papavas didn't understand these remarks, which appeared to have little connection to his houses.

When Papavas came to the United State he wanted to get away from the contractor-dominated Greek houses of his Athens home and to work as a modernist architect. To him this meant providing modern designs that blended functionality with the spaces in which clients could enjoy a modern, liberated family life. But it seemed that his ethical stance was being challenged by an invasion of ignorant professors!

Consoling himself with the knowledge that Greeks had invented civilization, he felt inspired to invent something himself to overcome this present crisis. And what he invented to solve the problem of unsaleable modernism was a new kind of "split level" residence, the difference in the Papavas version being that the "split" occurred in the vertical dimension rather than in the horizontal plane.

To deal with the aesthetic or "character" issue, Papavas decided that in the spirit of American compromise the exteriors of his Baton Rouge "Modern" houses had to be stylistically recognizable as French Provincial or French Colonial. Their roofs would have to be steeply pitched, with even the introduction of an occasional *Faux-Mansart* effect in response to upper storey accommodation. But what about the interior organization and arrangements, were they redesigned? The answer was "No": the interiors of what the architect called his "half-way" houses remained substantially indistinguishable from those of the original houses. As they say in Texas (and also seem to believe in Louisiana): "If it ain't broke, don't fix it".

Papavas' revised house images perfectly represent how many contemporary Americans develop a preference for adopting a sterile suburban life-style, one that is lived with the empty shell of a previous cultural reference. It would seem to be evidence, too, of schizophrenia, which is clearly the ailment that Nietzsche's modern man suffers from.

Another tale from the "home-front" concerns a Mid-Western architect we shall call Thomas, who is renowned for the distinctive character of his domestic architecture. His private houses reflect the influence of Frank Lloyd Wright's "Prairie Style", the difference being that the Thomas houses have a more genuine claim to the appellation "Prairie" than those of Wright.

One day a charming young couple, both doctors in their mid-30s, arrived at Thomas's office and asked him to design a house for them in their native State of Massachusetts. Thomas told them that, although flattered by their request, it wasn't really a practical proposition in terms of cost, taking into account the amount of travel to and from the East Coast, since he would have to insist upon supervising the construction of his design.

The young doctors were naturally disappointed. They had saved for several years to pay for the creation of their home, but they certainly understood how the architect's travel expenses would substantially reduce the amount of money left to spend on their house. As they talked, Thomas tried to come up with a solution to their problem. Eventually he had an idea. As it happened he had a good friend, an excellent modern architect, who lived and practiced in the Boston area. He could introduce the couple to Mac Stevens, who he was sure could design a very fine house for them. While it would not be a Thomas house, Stevens was very familiar with the landscape and climate of the East Coast, and his design might therefore be more appropriate. The points Thomas made were all perfectly reasonable and his attitude was completely professional.

The only trouble was that what the young doctors still had in mind was a Thomas house. They had never even heard of Stevens or seen any of his houses. We don't know what the couple were thinking as they left Thomas's office to return to Massachusetts. Eventually, however, they accepted that, as residents of Massachusetts, a Thomas house was financially beyond their reach. Within a couple of months they contacted Mac Stevens and commissioned him to design their new home. They were disappointed by his first sketches, simply because they bore no resemblance to a Thomas house. But they had come to like Stevens, and he seemed eager to interpret their ideas, giving them a design they could live with.

Construction took little more than a year, and the couple settled in. Stevens heard nothing from his clients for another two years. Then, suddenly, he was summoned to have cocktails with the two doctors, and he went to visit them one evening. They exchanged pleasantries over the first drink, then came a second, and still the conversation remained polite and unfocussed. Eventually, Stevens asked if they were having any problems with the house. The husband answered: "No, not really. But his wife quickly intervened to say that "Yes" there was just one thing.

She went on to explain: "You see, when we have guests, they naturally want a tour of our famous house. And most of them seem to like it quite a lot. But some are confused and they want to know what kind of a house this is." Stevens nodded but said nothing, so she continued: "For example, people say, well it's not Cape Cod, and it's not Colonial or Victorian. So just what kind of a house is it?" At that point Stevens suggested: "Well, clearly it won't help if you tell them its style is modern. So, why don't you just say: It's our kind of house?"

They thanked him for coming. Clearly, they had commissioned the wrong architect. What they had really wanted was a Thomas house, but instead they had bought a Stevens design. So, how could they possibly pretend that Stevens' design was their kind of house? But after a while, when they were quizzed about the pedigree of their home, they would answer: "Well, it's what we call our 'half-way house', because it's half the house we dreamed of and half the reality we inhabit".

There seems to be no escaping Nietzche's view that modern man has inherited "an interior to which there is no corresponding exterior, and an exterior to which there is no corresponding interior". Clearly, if modern man has become internalized the search for our missing externalization will be unsuccessful. Walter Benjamin describes not a "search" for externalization but "the concealment of its loss", substituting "habits for primary experience". In Italy, before Palladio, a farmer could "grow" his own farmhouse in a neighbouring field, as it were, spawning a *casa colonica* as part of Italy's *architettura* minore.

If we could reinvent today such a "lesser architecture", as Hilding Ekelund and his Finnish colleagues wanted to do, what would be its benefits? The first thing in its favour is that "lesser architecture" has a broad vocabulary of forms, including those that represent most architectural types. In addition lesser architecture lacks the capacity to confront all the difficulties we encounter in making theories of architecture. Those problems have their origins in the differentiations of style. This is perhaps another way of saying: "Where a continuous tradition of building exists, embracing types, forms and their making, there is no need for a theory of how to do those things. Tradition is a construct that depends on harnessing the potential of what is self-evident".

3 MEET THE PARENTS

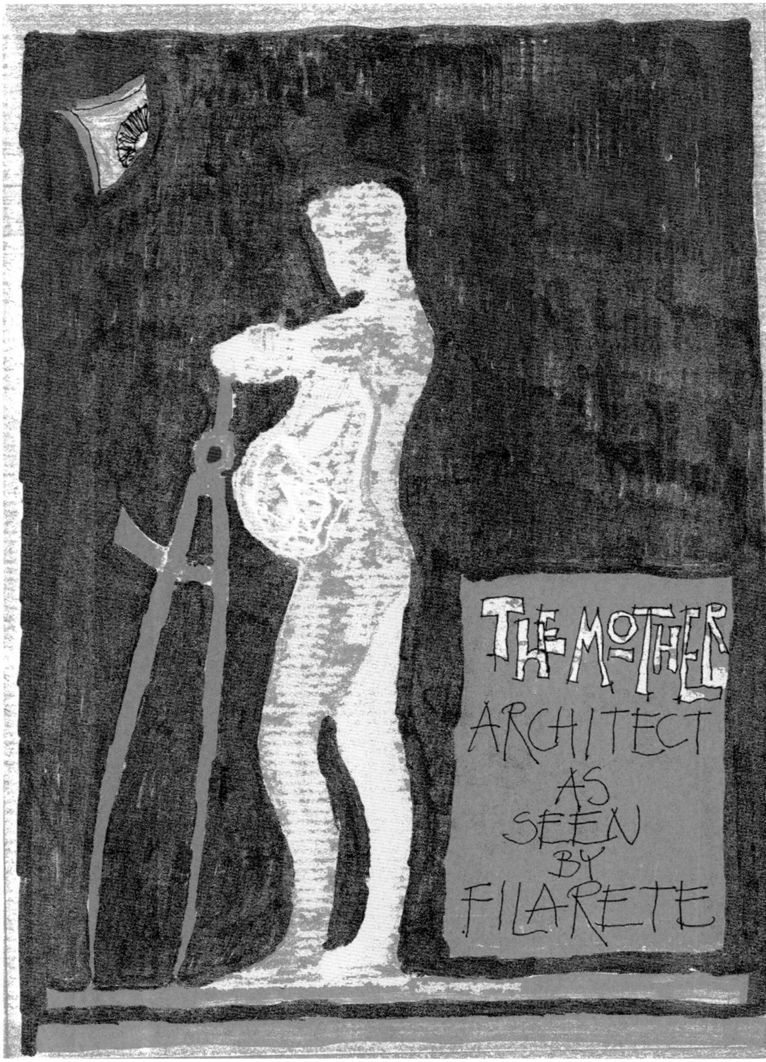
THE MOTHER
ARCHITECT
AS
SEEN
BY
FILARETE

MEET THE PARENTS | Matti K. Mäkinen

MQ: What do we mean by "a body" or "the body"? Is it our human body in the context of architectural space – the placement of our body within that space? Or is it the question of the architect's own body, acting to shape that space by providing "scale", by measuring his own form against its volumetric containment?

MKM: Body and Soul. Body and Mind. Mind and matter...Why is it so difficult to speak of the body without a complementary glance to the software controlling the body functions? Body without soul – whatever 'soul' means here – is only a dead body. Mentally a nobody. Only a heap of matter.

MQ: And what about the "the body of architecture" itself, the physical response in space and form to human physical, psychological and spiritual needs?

MKM: The first thing that comes to my mind is "body-building". Even the human body is not only something "given", it can also be built up, developed.

MQ: Does the "body of architecture" have a pronounced structure or formal anatomy that corresponds to human anatomy, which we find, for example, in Gray's celebrated 'ANATOMY'? Or is this notion of the "body of architecture" just a metaphor?

MKM: Or is architecture some body? Or rather a member in a larger context, an element for building a community, even a city? That needs more pondering. If you don't mind, I have to start "preaching".

When Protagoras said that man is the measure of all givens, did he speak of the dimensions of the human body or did he include the soul?

Measuring things in the plain 'body' dimension, we can reach a great part of the elementary aspects of building. We modulate our rooms to fit to the body, the height of our stair-steps and ladder-rungs and all the rest of the physical measures to easy and convenient use for man's purposes. We make our bricks taking into account the size and form of the bricklayer's hand, not to forget his movements when placing the bricks on the wall. We choose the materials in the walls and the openings according to man's need for shelter in the surrounding climate.

But 'body' is not only the physical structure with its parts, members, material substances and dimensions. The body is also the carrier of an appearance – and appearance is a transmitter of information. Many people love and even try to understand Sister Architecture through her looks.

When understanding architecture as mainly an art of appearances, our 'understanding' easily includes a good deal of underestimating. We throw glances after our Sister Architecture as if she were another girl in the street, trying to call the attention of not only potential lovers but also even well-to-do customers. Taking a look at the architectural magazines, you can see that this concentration on the sister's looks is not only a layman's girl-watching. Judging from the publicity, a lot of architects seem to follow a related line of thought. It's the looks that sell.

Who needs her intelligence, if she has astounding legs? "What is the beauty of a building to us today? The same as the beautiful face of a woman without spirit: something mask-like." (Nietzsche: *Menschliches, Allzumenschliches*, as quoted by Karsten Harries at the 7th Alvar Aalto Symposium)

After these remarks, we have to admit that the sister also has another body, invisible to the lay customer. In her bag, she carries a growing burden of architectural theory, or should we say theories. And most of these theories are built on this basic question: What is it about this thing called architecture?

Not to keep churning the same problem again and again, let me change my angle, reluctantly I admit, turning our gaze away from the pretty sister towards the family and the relatives. Mother Architecture I have mentioned already; who are the others?

One of the difficulties in defining architecture comes through a historical progress of chopping and re-chopping the original disciplines of human knowledge, creating ever-narrower sectors of study and action. Long ago, a special art of building was separated from the bulk of mere construction. The supervising masters of this art received the name of architects, 'the supreme builders'. The typical products of architecture were in the early times commissioned by the high and the mighty – and mainly they became monuments for money and power, planned for a timeless longevity. Coming to the time of our grandfathers, "a gentleman's house" could still be a typical programme for a commission. Passing by the well documented philanthropic factory owners of the late 1800s, we can generalise the topic by referring to the manifestoes of early Functionalism, showing paths to meet the needs of the lower classes and, as democracy gained a foothold, the 'ordinary people'.

For thousands of years, we thus had the monuments playing the role of forefathers to the family of Architecture. And then we had the houses, huts and shackles, the nameless patterns of shelters in the towns, the villages and the outskirts of the estates of the noblesse. The folk way of building, the vernacular (*verna* was the word for a female 'slave' who had been born on the Master's property), the architecture (mainly) without architects deserves actually much more attention than it has gotten during the long history of architecture. Just look at a town, any of them. No town consists of mere monuments, castles, palaces or even rich mans' houses. No way. Maybe the juices of real life brew behind those more or less unknown facades by unknown designers. Is it possible that in the long run the future dwells there.

This makes me think of the theme of the 9th Alvar Aalto Symposium in Jyväskylä. Architecture plays the role of the Elephant who lives a long time and never forgets – unlike the Butterflies which live only today and know nothing of yesterday. What is left as testimony to past empires and cultures, if not their architecture?"

What is not left, then? Where are the countless generations of butterflies, as some of the elephants still stand there, weather-bitten but there anyway? The nameless urban patterns of vernacular building are not designed for eternal life-spans, though this "evil" knowledge is scarcely mentioned at the roof-topping parties. What is the importance of this lesser esteemed category of the built environment? It's not only because the vernacular is the base matter for an eternal return of architecture, old and new. Maybe more important is the fact that the phenomenon we call architecture can only be called alive against a background, within a context of "mere" building.

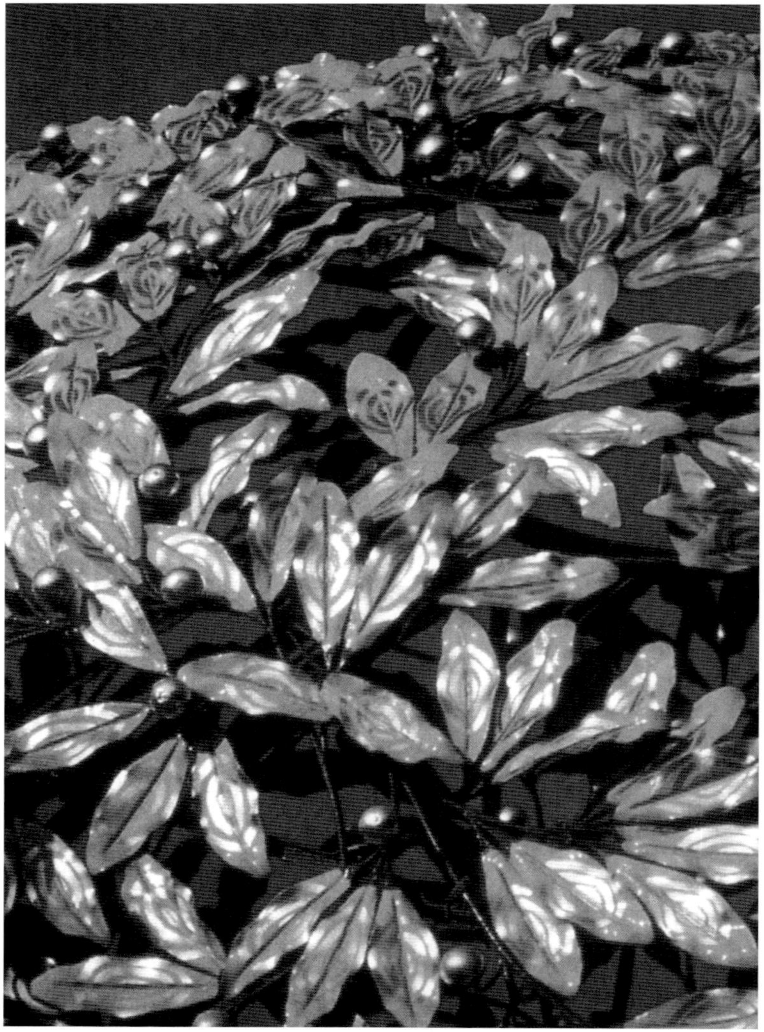

BUILDING A VISION BEYOND SEEING

Malcolm Quantrill

The essential distinction between the *Beaux Arts* discipline and those of the *Constructivist, de Stijl, l'Esprit Nouveau* and *Bauhaus* movements is that the latter set out determinedly to break with the past by formulating completely new design *languages.* While the "Classical Tradition" still lingered on in the *Ecole des Beaux Arts,* the advent of *Constructivism, de Stijl* and the *Bauhaus* swept from the "House of the Architect" those essential Classical rules of the *Taxis* (spatial order), the *Genera* (building elements or parts) and the *Symmetria* (the relationship of parts). This led Swiss architectural historian, Siegfried Giedion, to observe that by the mid-60s: "a certain confusion exists in contemporary architecture, as in painting, a kind of pause, even a kind of exhaustion. Everyone is aware of it. (But) We are still in the formation period of a new tradition, still at its beginning". [1]

Unshaken in his modernist stance, Giedion firmly believed that the main task facing contemporary architecture in the mid-60s was "the interpretation of a way of life valid for our period."

In *The Ethical Function of Architecture* (1997), Karsten Harries reports that, after three decades, the confusion Giedion had observed, which produced in turn post-modern, structuralist and deconstructive experiments, contemporary architecture has shown no sign of settling down to any consensus of form and expression that reflects some current *Zeitgeist.* Harries does not regret this, yet he finds himself unwilling to let go of Giedion's belief in modernism's main purpose; although he remains troubled by its two key notions and therefore asks:
(1) What does it mean to say that the task of architecture is one of interpretation?
(2) What exactly is the way of life that's valid for our period?

Harries argues that the first association we make with "interpretation" is its connection with literary texts. Does this suggest that works of architecture are like texts? Do they have a hermeneutic function? What tools of interpretation are available, then, to the architect? Should we, perhaps, consider

[1] Space, Time and Architecture, 3rd Edition, Zurich, 1967

architecture to consist of functionalist buildings that have been aesthetically dressed up?

In answering this second question, Harries challenges the capacity of our modern world, with its many differences of class, race, gender and religion, filled with confusion and contradiction, to offer any meaningful response that would give a universal fit? Perhaps the suspicions generated by postmodernism have made it impossible for architecture to any longer relate to Giedion's main task. He asks if it is possible to imagine a way of life that would be valid for everyman? Harries does not, however, want to give up on Giedion's modernist expectation and he suggests that perhaps architecture should continue to help us find our *place* and our way in this ever disorienting world? He therefore sets out to define what he calls the *ethical function* of architecture.

He explains that since the term "ethical" derives from "*ethos*", referring to a person's character, nature or disposition; or similarly to the *ethos* of a community, referring to the spirit that presides over its communal life; then *ethos* describes the way human beings exist in the world. Or, in Heidegger's terms, their way of *dwelling*. Therefore, by speaking of an "ethical function for architecture", Harries defines architecture's task as one of helping to articulate a common *ethos*. But can such an articulation enable us to locate and situate architecture in the world?

Harries thinks not. He cites Nikolaus Pevsner's observation that: "A bicycle shed is a building (while) Lincoln Cathedral is a piece of architecture" [2]. Strictly speaking, both shed and cathedral are buildings. But when the architect performs as a builder, it is customary to believe that he contributes something extra to the work. But how do we understand this "extra" quality? Pevsner suggests that architecture is "designed with a view to aesthetic appeal". Does this suggest that a work of architecture is essentially a functional object with an "aesthetic additive"? If so, perhaps we could decorate a number of utilitarian structures and label them as "architecture"?

Adolf Behne cites some late-nineteenth century examples of this approach in his *The Modern Functional Building*[3]. In the first chapter, "No Longer a House but a Facade", he describes the general condition of German public architecture at the end of the nineteenth century, where: "The plan was dominated by facades overloaded with decorative motifs, Heidelberg castles with a 'composition' irrelevant to their functional requirements. The most grotesque example: Ihne's Staatsbibliothek in Berlin, a concrete building that requires an artificial iron frame to support its sandstone Baroque façade, like a carnival mask!

Clearly, an 'aesthetic additive' cannot impart authenticity to 'foreign bodies'. That's important because it provides the lead into topic Number Two, 'Body'".

[2] *An Outline of European Architecture*, 1958
[3] Written 1923, published 1926

This "masking" of a building's essential bodily form gave rise in the 1970s to Venturi's significant Postmodern provocation that "architecture is either a duck or a decorated shed"[4]. The coining of the term "decorated shed" again connects us back through time to the role of decoration in historical architecture while, at the same time, granting license for the distinctly playful use of decoration that characterizes much Post-modernism architecture. As Harries points out, this very playfulness had been anticipated by Giedion with his suggestion that modern archi-tecture had already given way to: "....a kind of playboy architecture an architecture treated as playboys treat life, jumping from one sensation to another and quickly bored with everything."[5].

Giedion clearly hoped that this "playboy architecture" would prove to be nothing but a passing fancy, but the end of the century and the millenium have merely confirmed the persistence of a sort of "romantic orgy" that has displaced the puritanical canon of functionalist modernism. Perhaps, after all, this desire to avoid the boredom of repe-tition and seek out instead ephemerally provocative digressions is symptomatic of our time and space?

Harries supports the idea that postmodernism follows modernism in much the same way as Mannerism followed Renaissance or Rococo followed Baroque, suggesting that both modernism and postmodernism can be considered as architectural *styles* that rival the great styles of the past. Indeed, such arguments have already been advanced, proposing that the work of Wright, Le Corbusier, Mies van der Rohe and other leading modernists had put an end to the stylistic chaos of the late nineteenth century, but those arguments have certainly been undermined by architectural developments in the second half of the twentieth century. Harries therefore cautions that: "…linear accounts of the history of architecture as a succession of important aesthetic events are of course much too simple. We are still not done with modernism. And how could we be? For what do we mean by 'modern' and 'modernism'. Does not 'modern' refer to a period extending to and including the very present?

'Modernism' names an ideology that affirms what is thought to be in tune with the spirit or essence of our own period, in tune with science and technology, with modernity it defines itself in opposition to what went before, to traditions that retained their hold even as they had become anachronisms."

This might seem to be an appropriate point to review the concept of *Type* and the typological approach to design, in relation to both "modernity" and the notion of an "ethical function" for architecture. Let us first consider the use of the *Type* as a model for architectural form in the design process, the practice of using and repeating a building form concept that has proved its

[4] Venturi, Scott Brown and Izenour, *Learning from Las Vegas: The Forgotten Symbolism of Architectural Form*, 1977
[5] *Space, Time and Architecture*

effectiveness and formal value over the centuries. This involves reference to such simple particulars of architectural compositioas "the shed" (better known, perhaps as "the barn") and its more sophisticated interpretation as the aisled *basilican* church (or barn), since the difference between them is characteristically not one of form but of scale and volume (size).

In mediaeval rural England, as in other countries during that period, the difference between the barn and the parish church was mainly one of size and detail. The barn, being a functional building, has less detail, less fuss, less enrichment. But its form often exhibited the same basic type as that of the church, including even a higher, wider central space (nave) accompanied by lower, narrower side aisles. Perhaps it is not beyond the bounds of speculation to recognize in this symbiosis of barn and church, that very evidence of accommodation Professor Harries seeks in applying his test of an "ethical function" to architecture. Would not the similarity of church-form and barn-form confirm, both conceptually and practically, the relationship between a "storage vessel" for grain and other foodstuffs, located in the space of the workplace and the span of the workweek, and a similar but distinguishing "storage vessel" capable of gathering (harvesting) souls on the day appointed in Genesis to rest from work and the manifestation of God's "Saving Grace" on the Sabbath.

Taking the barn type as his model, Alvar Aalto explored the symbiotic relationship between the Council Chamber at Säynätsalo Town Hall in Central Finland, designing the form of the Chamber ceiling and its supporting trusses to echo the roof geometry commonly found in traditional Finnish barns. The result was that those local farmers who have been elected as Council Members are accommodated in a barn-like Council Chamber, which is itself accommodating of their day-to day working *ethos.* Aalto's humanist gesture here seems to offer a truly positive example of architecture's "ethical function" in action. Certainly, in much of his work from the mid-30s onwards, Aalto "furnished", "clothed", or "detailed" his modernism in such a way that it would be symbiotic with the two Finnish cultures of the twentieth century – the one historic and traditional, and the other in process of modernist evolution.

Harries provocatively suggests that: ... "the important aesthetic event that has given today's architectural landscape its contours would seem to be postmodernism."

But should architecture be viewed and valued principally in terms of "aesthetic events"? Is it at all conceivable that such a role could be compatible with its "ethical function"? Aalto's Council Chamber for Säynätsalo Town Hall is anything but an aesthetic event. Indeed, Harries goes on to suggest that it is precisely because postmodernism was, from its very beginnings, overly concerned with the creation of aesthetic events that it "went astray". The quality we should surely seek to cultivate in the architectural enterprise is *not* its eventfulness but its RESONANCE.

If we review the mainline modernists and postmodernists, Aalto stands out as a somewhat "reluctant hero" who, in spite of outbursts of personal egotism in his later years, was never inclined to stage an "aesthetic event" or to deliver a "cultural statement". During the last decade of his life, he was distinctly uncomfortable with the attention-getting "shock tactics" of postmodernists. After his early buildings of the 1920s his interest shifted substantially to the formation of new and habitable interior spaces of modernism. Of course, in his designs of the early-20s he eagerly followed the Romantic (or Nordic) Classic style that was then the prevaling mode of architectural expression throughout Scandinavia. We might say, in Harries' terms, that Aalto was anxious to show himself to be part of Scandinavia's "regional contours". Interestingly, the Romantic-Classic style fits perfectly with the notion of the "decorated shed", since it focussed on the use of simple classical volumes – the cube, the cylinder, the circular or square "doughnut", etc – a range of basic "warehouses" or "sheds", which were then decked out in skimpy, bikini-like Neo-Classical "dress"

As he demonstrated in the Säynätsalo Council Chamber, Aalto's work is evidence of an "architecture of accommodation": his accommodation of architecture's "ethical function" lies principally within the interiors of his buildings. When we visit an Aalto building, it is immediately apparent that his very sense of "interiority" speaks clearly of such an accommodation. His exterior forms, on the other hand are often arbitrarily or aggressively shaped, even lumpen – perhaps somewhat like the coarse, uneven walls of mediaeval barns or castles, or the rough surfaces of *l 'archittura minore*, providing equivalent protection for farm produce or a vulnerable populace.

But Aalto, who was a lover of historical examples, particularly if they were found in Italy, always sought after what was fundamental in architecture: he saw the Renaissance as the crowning manifestation of *Baukunst* ("architecture" or the "*art* of building"). But equal with that sense of art (*Kunst*) Aalto had from an early age, in 1923 when he was just 25, identified himself with the down-to-earth tradition of *l'architettura minore*, that "lesser architecture" which had flourished through the ages in the Italian provinces, particularly those of Tuscany and Umbria. From that Italian tradition Aalto learned what we might call the "directness of example": in other words, when precedent fails to offer solutions to the problem at hand it is necessary to invent an alternative solution with contemporary or *modern* means.

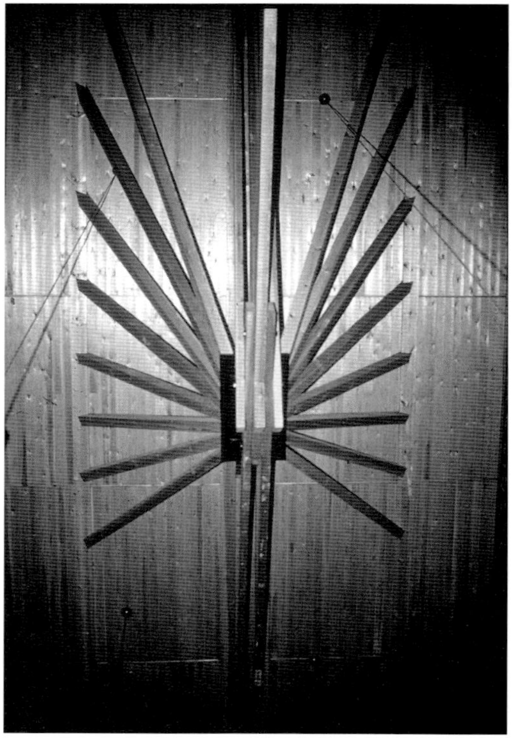

It might be helpful here to compare and contrast the modernist "interpretations" of Le Corbusier with those of Alvar Aalto. Corbusier's 5-Points developed in *Vers Une Architecture* (1923) outline five innovative freedoms for space and form:
(1) the plan to be free of the structure
(2) the façade to be free from the structure
(3) *pilotis* that free (lift) the building from the ground
(4) the freedom of the façade to accommodate continuous horizontzl windows
(5) *le toit-jardin* (roof garden under the open sky).

In reality, of course, these so-called "freedoms" constituted new *rules of composition* So we might say that the modernism of Le Corbusier is based in part on a revised system of academic ordering, the purpose of which is to generate and develop new architectural forms.

Today we view the recent "cultural events" of postmodern architecture, with its confusion of forms and styles, as chaotic and anarchic expressions. While they may represent uncertainty about our culture, language and meaning, they cannot at the same time be construed as manifestations of Harries "common ethos". It may well be that the situation in architecture and the arts between the beginning of Cubism (1907) and the end of the 1920s was viewed by some of its contemporaries as being similarly chaotic and anarchic. If we consider the diversity of work produced by Wright and Rietveldt, Loos and Gropius, Perret and Le Corbusier, we will find there was no one clear direction for modernism to take.

Le Corbusier's idea was to instil logical method into this stylistic vacuum, to develop rationality and order out of its apparent chaos. It is significant that he began by tackling the problem through the art of painting, working with Ozenfant to resist the vibrant experiments of Picasso and René Magritte with the pale silhouettes and shadows of *Le Purism*. Purism was, after all a regulated academic art: one might even say that its rules were essentially classical because it relates to French academicism in the strictest sense. Not surprisingly, therefore, the rules of Purism found their way into Le Corbusier's first excursion into architectural theory, *Vers Une Architectur* (1923) (emphatically translated into its English title as *Towards a* NEW *Architecture*)

The hallowing of the industrial object, the *ikon* that provides the credo for Purist art – all those pressed glass bottles and wine-goblets – is taken up and elaborated in *Vers Une Architecture*. In Le Corbusier's modernism, architecture is not the model for architecture: instead the powerful

American grain elevator, the Transatlantic liner, the aeroplane and the racing car – are substituted for traditional architectural typologies. Clearly, it is Le Corbusier's intent to move architecture out of its fixed traditional abode, out of its static place (*locus*), even out of its own house (*domus*) – "The House of Architecture" and project it into a world of mobile forces and images. He advocated an architecture based for it's "aesthetic appeal" on industrial imagery and its metaphors. There was only one obstacle in his path, but it was a rather substantial one.

When we return to Harries' difficulty in accepting Giedion's main task for architecture (1968) as "the interpretation of a way of life that is valid for our time" we discover that Le Corbusier seems to have lacked the tools necessary to achieve such an interpretation. He may have thought that the metaphors for functional modernism were the transatlantic liner or the American grain silo, but his interpretations of such concepts are quite unconvincing. For architecture is neither an ocean liner nor an aeroplane, any more than it is a "*machine a habiter*". A metaphor may *stand in* for a "building idea". Or a building may, in the literary or textural sense, interpret a metaphor. But a metaphor cannot actually represent the "building idea", and the proposition that "a house is a machine for living" is a good example of this kind of misconception.

It is significant that *Le Purism* took its *ikons* not from industry itself, not from actual industrial processes, but from products of industry. This gap between the image and the reality was transferred by Le Corbusier from *Le Purism* to *Vers une Architecture*. That opened the door to the suggestion that the paintings produced by the Purists (Le Corbusier and Ozenfant) were not truly *modern* works at all, but works firmly rooted in the formulaic tradition of Neo-Classicism. Perhaps they are disguised, but only thinly so, by their lack of symmetry, but their elements are essentially classical, especially in their formality and in their representation of the "static" condition. The objects depicted in Purist paintings are fixed in space and time. In Purism there is no attempt to engage the essence of modernism, no interest in even flirting with the very spirit of the "modern *movement*".

It was Marcel Duchamp who led the way in capturing modernism's spirit of movement in space. In *Nude Descending a Staircase*, and *King and Queen Surrounded by Swift Nudes*, plus half a dozen other pictures painted between 1911 and 1913, Duchamp made machine-inspired movement the essence of what was modern in twentieth century painting. For all its energy and flurry, Futurist painting is no match for Duchamp's unique synthesis of human form and machine-motion.

In *The Ethical Function of Architecture*[6], Harries cites the contemporary American painter, Frank Stella and quotes the artist's view of his aesthetic goal: "I always get into arguments with people who

[6] pp. 16–18

want to retain old values in painting, the humanistic values that they always find on the canvas. If you pin them down they usually end up asserting that there is something there besides the paint. (But) my painting is based on the fact that only what can be seen is actually there. It really is an object. All I want anyone to get out of my paintings is the fact that you can see the whole idea without any confusion... *What you see is what you see.*"

Clearly, Stella does not intend anyone looking at his painting in search of some hidden meaning. Or, as Harries puts it: *Its presence should not be haunted by absence.* From Stella's statements Harries distils what he calls "a first description of the aesthetic object", to which he assigns four characteristics:

(1) The aesthetic object should not *mean* but *be.*
(2) The aesthetic object should present itself as a whole.
(3) The aesthetic object demands aesthetic distance.
(4) The aesthetic object promises to put us at one with ourselves.

Harries maintains, however, that we cannot begin to understand architecture as an "aesthetic object" within the meaning of these characterizations. He affirms that buildings and their elements have to carry meanings if they are to function: "houses have to look like houses, doors like doors, works of architecture should therefore *mean*, not just *be.* Also, buildings do not normally present themselves in their totality: we experience them, rather, from different and separate points of view, from different angles. From inside or outside, from front or back, a building opens up and unfolds, revealing only part of itself at any one time. In addition, our use of buildings is not easily reconciled with maintaining that required "aesthetic distance": our comings and goings within and through buildings, our need to renew them, to modify and transform them, speaks more of an intense *involvement* with the fabric than of *remoteness* or *detachment.* As for that promise to "put us at one with ourselves", it seems rather that a successful building conspires to lift us out of ourselves,. setting us off on a journey of exploration through a world that is beyond our experience and therefore outside the material limits of architecture, in other words "beyond those comforting memories of the womb".

But that is the very realm Frank Stella forbids his objects to embrace. For him there is nothing beyond the appearance of the object, in his case the "painting". He has no tolerance of a "hidden meaning", which can be sought out and disclosed. He insists instead that: "What you see is what you see". That's all very well for Mr Stella, but we cannot pretend that is very poetic. Also, if it is not necessary to seek beyond the surface of an object, to think about its undertow, to excavate for some underlying message, then we might well ask: "Is this object intelligible?" "Does it present a challenge to the intellect, a provocation to which the intelligent, curious spectator must respond?" If the ethical function of architecture is that of "helping to articulate a common ethos", what level of intelligence, of intellectual enquiry, should it aim to promote in that "articulation"? It would seem appropriate that a dialog should be initiated to underly or to inhabit that common ethos. The ethical function of an architecture that would articulate such a common ethos should surely have a supporting role. I am not referring here to material or structural supports of a building, but to the forms, spaces and the quality of daylight captured and framed by those supports.

Perhaps, in this sense, architecture's "ethical function" must be to ask more questions for which it can ever find answers. For example, in enclosing space, in assuming its nurturing feminine character of "womb", architecture should promise a world beyond that of enclosure, a speculative life beyond the security of "womb-space". In other words, in articulating "a common ethos", it is necessary for architecture to delimit its structural, formal and spatial constraints. The winners of the prestigious Pritzker Prize for 2001, the Swiss architects of London's new *Tate Modern Gallery*, Herzog and de Meuron, speak of making architecture *not* more exclusive as a commodity, but allowing it to become more inclusive. As Herzog explained in a recent National Public Radio interview: "There are many things around us that are not normally considered to belong to architecture. We try to bring some of them in, to include them and make them part of a larger whole."

But would such a new comprehensiveness increase the commonality of the ethos? The answer must be "not necessarily so". Robert Pinsky, American Poet Laureate for most of the 1990s, spoke recently at Texas A&M University about the process of making a poem. He described in detail how he collects *words*, *images* (about the subject of the poem), and the varied *connections* or *associations* that come to mind and, in turn, generated *ideas* about the poem he is trying to shape in his mind. Not all those words, images, connections or ideas would find their way into the final poem, but in the process of exploring the poem's shape and character, its rhythms and its landscape of language, every possible aspect of its form and flow should be reviewed. Herzog and Pinsky support the need for a truly comprehensive search or "research".

In a sense both archtect and poet are trying to ensure that "no stone is left unturned" But the approach of both creators – the architect to the structure and form of a building and the poet to the constructs and reverberations of his poem – involves a scanning and sifting of the material from which the *thing* will be formed and refined, selecting what is appropriate, puzzling interesting or provocative and rejecting the ultimately arbitrary, balancing provocative elements against a sure foundation and a substantial framework of reference.

The reason for introducing the poet Pinsky and the process of making poems into this discussion is to get rid of the notion that the making and enjoyment of architecture is centered on some ill-conceived, unique aesthetic *persona*, an existence not shared with other creative *genre*. Instead I want to join Bachelard in making the case for architecture to possess a truly poetic existence. After all, a poem is not only a measure of words or a museum of images – the 14-line sonnet or the 4-line *haiku* – a poem exists beyond its diminutive size on the page, in a book or suspended in the air, where it may be confined within a few words or lines, or take just a couple of minutes to read. A poem may embrace metaphor, but it is not only an interpretation of metaphor; its fundamental cadence and its supporting rhythms take us beyond the poem, both in our memories and through projections into times and spaces of which we have no previous knowledge or experience.

Our hearts, and with them our minds are also in tune with the interiors of those extraordinarily harmonious French and Italian Romanesque abbey churches and their supremely static cloisters. The supernatural seems undoubtedly present in those breathtaking spaces, as though they were designed not by men but through some "divine intervention". Such Romanesque architecture suggests that its architect, or master mason, had become lost in the contemplation of his architectural goal and surrendered all his skill and cleverness to a vision of eternal harmony. What he seems to have gained through that vision was a divine facility which allowed him to manipulate space and material, endowed him with an ability to create passageways between our present reality and an idealized perception of form; and through those channels we are conducted into relationships of which we have no pre-knowledge.

In his final book, *The Projective Cast* (1995), the English historian and critic Robin Evans (1944–93), discusses the very different relationship the Renaissance architect had with the buildings he designed:

"For Wöfflin the forms of centralized buildings contained directly assayable sense, the cumulative import of which betrayed the mood of the age. For Wittkower, on the other hand, the supporting documentation was the repository of legitimate meanings. Meanings lay behind forms. Forms were signs. The legibility of these signs was always at risk because it was based on cultural conventions, not universal psychology. The architectural historian stood over them as guardian and expositor, protecting and perpetuating their meanings. The symbolic in *Architectural Principles* is the authorized. Things are what they are said to be. By this definition, meaning is constructed through stipulation, and on the authority of those who recorded and propogated it ...the story of Renaissance architecture was henceforth to be the story of the incorporation of prescribed symbols into monuments. A fascinating ecology of words and things was mapped out: an ecology that, viewed from within its own frame of reference, gave the impression of being entirely self-sufficient. The point is, it requires an act of complicity between the historian and his sources to maintain this vision within the frame."

Peter Eisenman is part of the Wittkower legacy, his architecture depends upon texts, although these texts purport to have historical, literary or genealogical foundations. Certainly, Eisenman sets out to construct elaborate webs of intellectual speculation. Indeed, one might perhaps be reminded of the literary labyrinths of Jorge Luis Borges. But there is an important distinction between the representations of Borges and those of Eisenman. For Eisenman's cultural games exhibit surface effects that are conclusive in themselves. Eisenman's architecture is constructed as a kind of arcane, intellectual game, some sort of *Glass-Bead Game*, only it is basically two-dimensional and therefore lies outside the essential reverberations of experiential architectural space.

In a typical Borges story, we find its author contemplating the task of constructing and writing an encyclopaedic work, but he gets sidetracked from the actual project, seeking instead some alternative means of realising it. Rather than writing the book itself, he decides, as it were, to *deconstruct* it. This he does by "inventing" a journal review of such a volume, fictionalising the editor, the contextual material and, of course, all the appropriate quotations from the text. In this way the scholar's task was moved from that of a purely literary construction to something akin to Kant's *Critique of Pure Reason*. In architectural terms, we might think of this as cutting away the underpinning and the scaffolding to reveal an anatomical section through the building's aedicule and its innermost fabric.

Such a fictional slice through a "work of fact", *une tranche de la vie vraie* cut from a non-existent book, offers the skeleton of an imaginary text. It provides both the construct of a literary fantasy and the framework for a fantastic architecture that is clothed in an intangible façade. Perhaps Eisenman is himself attempting to emulate the Borgesian technique of "project avoidance"? On the other hand, we might view this Borges story as offering a parody of Eisenman's approach to problem-solving.

In architecture, the reception of surface signs and symbols – or "you see what you see" – should not be the full story. In other words, what those limitations present falls short of a full revelation of Baukunst. The *in depth* qualities of the "common ethos", those layers of meaning concealed beneath the surface, only become evident through perceptions of and insights into what remains invisible and intangible. Of course, the properties of architecture, its materiality, its structure, its form, its luminosity, all contribute to "building" its *externalisation*. But it is what is wrapped up and enfolded within architecture's planes and surfaces that offers the keys to its hidden realms and dimensions. Beyond what we now see of a building lies both what we may have already seen, and what we may never see.

That "What you see is what you see" is a slogan for the dullard. If dullards are the typical citizens of Harries' "common ethos", if these are our clients, what point would there be in making an architecture for them? For architecture should be inventive and provocative, conspiring to capture beneath its surfaces a spirit that is beyond the geometry of its immediate and superficial presence. And when all has been said, architecture exists *not* between the pages of a text but between the walls that define its spatial characteristics, that fit and lock it in its place.

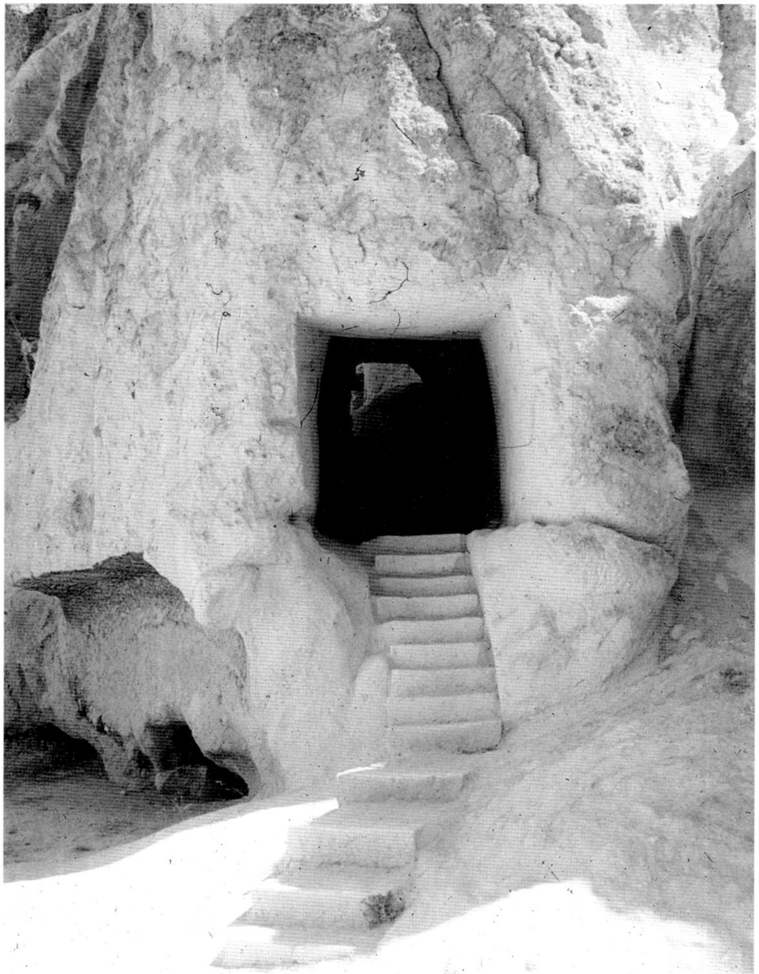

HOUSE AND HOME – BODY AND SOUL

Matti K. Mäkinen

In der Mitte aller Ferne
steht dies´Haus,
drum hab´es gerne [1]
Herman Broch: *Inscriptio*

My home is my castle. My home is my house. My home is my apartment. My home is my nest. Which one would be your choice?

The creator of the Finnish garden city of Tapiola, Heikki von Hertzen, wrote in the late 1940s a pamphlet opening new vistas for Finland's national housing policy: "A Home or a Barrack for our Children" is my free translation of the title. Today, an updated edition would be useful. Perhaps the name could be "A Home or a Flat for our Children".

The use of language is rather careless when it comes to the differences between the concepts of 'house' and 'home'. One example could be the salesmen in the real estate business, who gladly advertise "homes" for sale or rent, when what they are actually selling or renting are houses and apartments. These are the physical frames, where the dwelling functions are located, according to our way of thinking. And what could better serve the business of the home-sellers. *We are right in the heart, close to the warmth of the hearth.* Very nice.

The home is a conceptual oddball. Its dimensions span from the Heideggerian philosophies of being thrown to dwell in the world, all the way down to the warm and intimate safety of a nest. The home is located in an apartment or a house. Yet it is not the same thing. "Houses are commonly attributed an economic value, an exchange value, an aesthetic value and a use value. In addition to

[1] My clumsy translation: "In the middle of all remotes stands this House, thus love it."

these, a home is usually attributed a sentimental and symbolic value".[2] A home is not only a bulding with walls and a roof and spaces, it involves also the people who live there. And not only the family, members of the household, but also a number of others, from the closest neighbours and their dog to the mailman and the woman selling at the corner shop. From these circles the home expands to the dimensions of a neighbourhood, the home town, home region and home country. As the situation is now, the idea of world citizens is not so distant as it was only a few decades ago. Here we come across the dialogue between the local and the global, right in our own backyard.

Isn't there something old-fashioned in this idea of a home? At least in the architectural world, 'home' seems to be a half-forgotten concept. But the architects do not worry; they are busy enough designing buildings, houses and blocks of flats, marketware for the real estate business. Is it possible, that the word 'home' evokes images that seemingly do not offer challenges to use the sharp edge of modern design? Something too soft and relaxed, cosy and homely. Even the interest of the dwellers moving in seems to be limited to selecting from ready-made products offered by the home decoration industry. The dreams come true in contact with the dearest people, a happy life accompanied by new window curtains, bedlinen and luxurious pillows.

A frequent task for the children in the kindergarden is to make a drawing of 'home'. We can only wonder where it is that children always pick up the same images of an ideal home. There it stands, a detached house, of course, with a pitched roof and a chimney in the middle sending some curling smoke towards the blue sky. A radiant yellow sun up on the left, some steps at the entrance and Mama standing there with open arms, an apron and a broad smile. We architects could ask ourselves, whence the kids get these ideas, although the real home can be a block of flats with a flat roof and grey concrete element walls. This must be a persistant continuity, reflecting the myth of eternal return,[3] picked up from the illustrations in the fairy-tale books. Do we learn anything of the human mind by studying these day-dreams from the days of innocence?

Some decades later, when the time is ripe for a return, these children visit their old places to catch some of the old atmosphere. In many cases it would be more advisable not to make the journey. New developments have rolled over their childhood landscape leaving few clues to support their memories. The actual house may still be there, but their home will have vanished. Even the tree that marked the dog's grave has been removed long ago. So much of the nostalgia, the memories and the sorrowful returns to a non-place that once was the place of home.

[2] Lawrence Roderick: "The Meaning and Use of Space", *Journal of Architectural and Planning Research*, Vol. 8, number 2.

[3] I owe the phrasing to Mircea Eliade, *Le Mythe de l'eternel retour*, 1949

A home is not only a depository of the family's and the generation's memories. As long as there still is life, the life functions fill the house. A home is associated with the soft paths of feeling, effecting both mind and body, while the house represents the hard, physical, economic and technical aspects. The house represents... indeed, what? This is no longer a story of the body and mind of architecture, and I leave it to the next letter.

If the human being has a home somewhere, it is where he/she is familiar with the environment. (Eeva-Liisa Manner, Finnish writer).

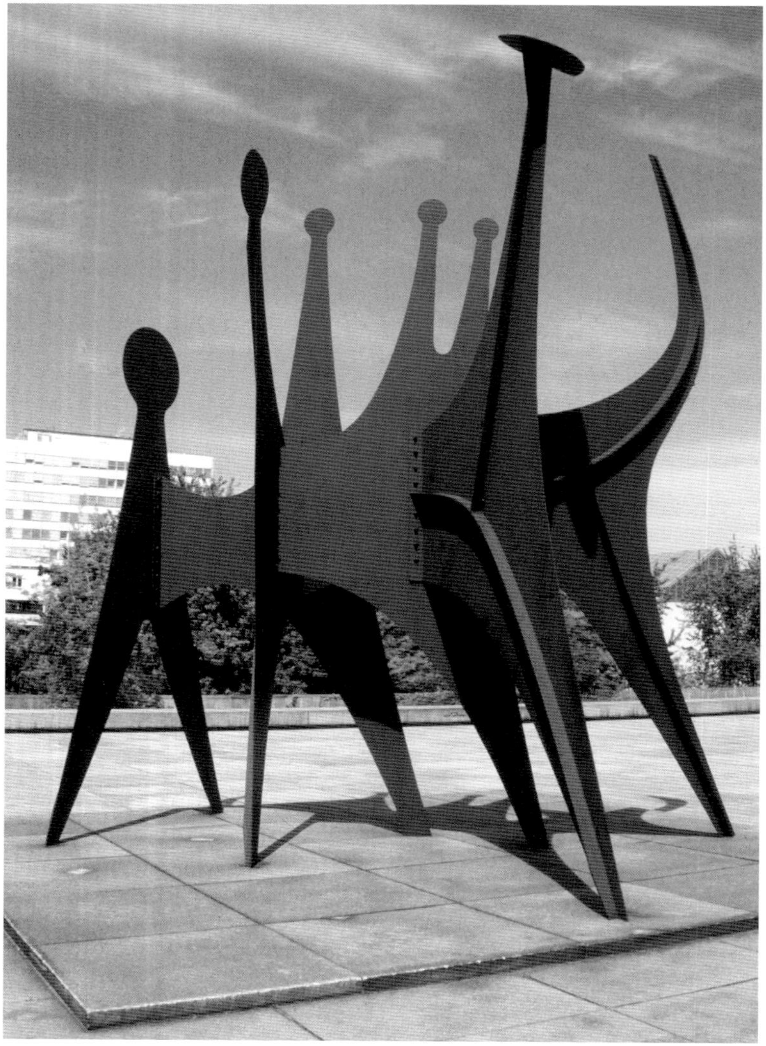

ELEPHANT AND BUTTERFLY

Matti K. Mäkinen

Architecture is an Elephant – in a world made of language.

I begin by quoting the Finnish architect Kristian Gullichsen "The elephant is strong and wise and endowed with a splendid memory. The elephant is ponderous and finds it difficult to change direction in a split second, unlike a butterfly. The butterfly for its part is usually pretty but lacks memory, because its life is so short and it has little to remember. An elephant should not be treated like a butterfly to safeguard it from undue suffering."

This definition caught attention and after three years, it was taken up again. The 9th International Alvar Aalto Symposium adopted the theme "Permanence and Change in Architecture", and the Elephant experienced a revival: "Elephants live a long time and never forget – unlike a butterfly which lives only today and knows nothing of yesterday".

MQ: This Alvar Aalto event is of particular interest to me, because the source of *Permanence and Change* as a conference theme was embodied in a symposium I chaired at Texas A+M University (1989). The proceedings of that symposium were later published jointly by the Center for Advancement of Studies in Architecture (CASA) and Texas A+M University Press under the title *Constancy and Change in Architecture* (1991), in other words twelve years before the Alvar Aalto Symposium of 2003. I just want to keep the record straight about the origins of "permanence" and "change" in architecture, while conceding that the metaphor of *elephant versus butterfly* is Kristian Gullichsen's invention...

MKM: Here we see a good example of the eternal return in the realm of architecture....But let me go on...

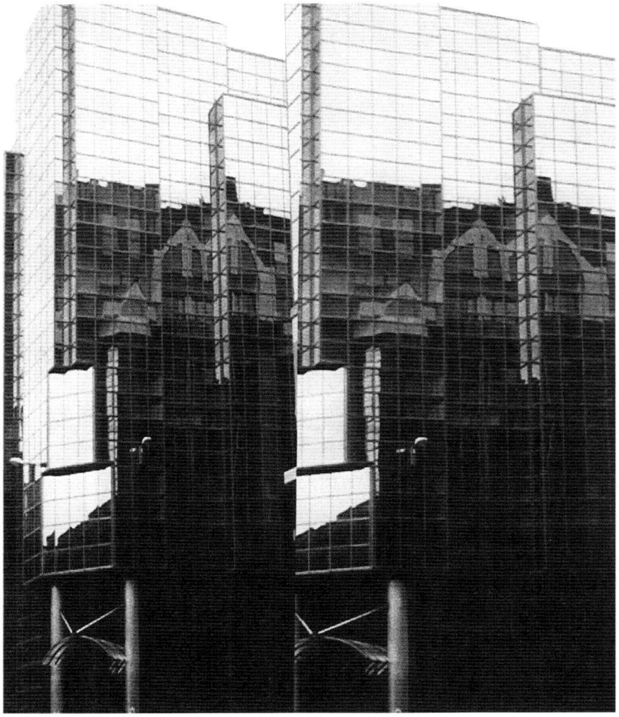

This theme leads us back to the role of architecture versus mere building. If the monuments are the elephants of architecture, meant to carry their memories over centuries, so vernacular buildings might be the dancing butterflies, coming and going, living their day and forgotten tomorrow, replaced by new generations. We could think that – whatever the degree of the elephants' suggested memory – the memory of the butterfly is genetically deposited and reappears with renewing generations. This way, the light movements of the butterfly represent an eternity, while a dead elephant is just a dead elephant when its time is over. And the same holds true for the eternal return of the butterflies of nameless vernacular in comparison to the renowned elephants of architecture.

British cultural critic Roger Connah warned me against the excessive use of metaphors: in his view they are too common in writings about architecture. Indeed, as I started to memorize some of the best known definitions of architecture, I recognised a richness of metaphorical expressions shining through. There is presently an exhibition in London on zoomorphic architecture.[1] In this connection, we can also take a side glance to the various examples of anthropomorphic architecture, or the fish-like image at Barcelona's Vila Olimpica by Frank Gehry, not to mention Santiago Calatrava's art museum at Milwaukee, likened to a whale's tail. Is it possible that our beloved architecture is so indefinable, that we cannot manage to explain it without a reference to something outside the discipline? One of the best known metaphors is Le Corbusiers' vision of "the masterly play of light…". With a second thought, we grasp that light does not play anything, anywhere. It is human perception that leads to an interpretative idea of playing. One of the guaranteed metaphor-free definitions comes from Louis Kahn's account that "Architecture *is*".

To return to the zoo of architecture, I cannot forget those wooden horses. Architecture plays a wooden horse maybe more frequently than we think; a Trojan Horse, carefully designed to smuggle a variety of items. To build a better world, or only a vision of it?

A Trojan Horse? No, not only one, but a whole herd of them. Some horses I even call by name. At a first glance I can see at least: Transparency, Solidity, Real Estate, Sustainability, Life cycle, Futuricity and Heritage; all of them prepared to pass the checkpoints with their masked cargo. When I see them in action, I can use my magic x-ray eyes and discern some of the secrets behind their masks. Let's have a closer look.

Transparency passes first. The contraband inside consists of the glass boxes of modern architecture, the prevailing hallmark of world-wide business culture. The three most effective arguments used in advertising this product of architecture are based on economy, ecology and the unique character of

[1] "Zoomorphic" exhibition at the Victoria and Albert Museum, London, Nov.2003-Jan 2004. Also, the exhibition on animalism in art, "Animal and Man" at the Knighthood House, Tallinn, Jan–April 2004.

this heroic modernism. Last but not least comes transparency as the democratic message of corporate openness reflected from the facades. Indeed, reflected, if you can see anything through the mirroring reflections of shaded glass. Can you see the economy of cooling and heating, scrubbing and cleaning to secure the imaginary transparency? Can you see the ecology of energy consumption? The unique personal touch of thousands of other glass boxes all over the world, the economy of standardization achieved as all of them tell the same story, carry the same symbols of professing to the faith of a globalised market ideology? The uniqueness resembling that of a group of Japanese businessmen, cloned in their dark business uniforms?

Solidity carries in his stomach the assumption of solid and rational knowledge, the entire scale from the laboratories of top level science to the practical know-how of a construction team foreman. We build for longevity. We build upon the grounds of latest research and knowledge. Pity that some problems still occur in keeping the rain out and the warmth in. But these are only practical misfortunes, more important is that we *know*. After thousands of years of construction work, we have learnt our lessons. "Is this really so?" some layman might ask. The answer is given by Bruce Sterling: "There might be a world that has a true reality. But because we are in a world that's made of language, we'll never ever get to that place from here."[2]

Real Estate enters the market at full gallop. Her name reveals that she is the same breed as *Solidity*. Her name is only the first layer of her mask. Her burden does not weigh so much, the material consists mainly of very fluid matter, like capital investments, the anonymity of the investors, that of the clients, even the users to-be. The Emperors' new clothes make up part of the contents. Through her swift movements, *Real Estate* covers large areas, leaving – as her name promises – deep and visible footprints. The vision fades as swiftly as it appeared. What was *real* in this process? You don't have to search for evidence with a magnifying glass, at least the Estate is there, only completely turned into a new shape. "The magic touch of money?" the layman asks, raising his hat toward the direction from where the horse had come.

We don't need a detailed description of the other sisters' capacities. A red thread of resemblance goes through the family tree. The time has come to ask: "What has all of this to do with architecture?" More than you think, I would answer. The spirit of the time might be a common denominator. But before the final conclusion, we read again some wise words by Bruce Sterling:

"There is no such thing as 'truth' ...There is only language. There's no such thing as a 'fact'. There is no truth or falsehood, just dominant processes by which reality is socially constructed."

[2] Bruce Sterling, *Zeitgeist*, New York, Bantam Books, 2000

Sigfried Giedion defines architecture as *"an interpretation of the way of life valid for our period"*. If we accept this, the next question is, how can we follow this kind of a definition in our daily work? What is the way of life valid for our period? And how long is a "period"? Is it long enough to make a road map for the slowly moving elephant of architecture?

I don't know if we should feel sorry or not, but our contemporary architecture is more easily compared to the butterflies, moving swiftly, some reaching the skies, seeking attention through their rhythmic, graceful swings, not to forget the golden sunshine playing on their colourful wings. And some others seek shelter in a lower profile, closer to the ground. Anyway, all of them have to hit the ground when their day is over.

In his book *Dream Society*, Rolf Jensen describes the idea of development through the spectacles of business culture.[3] He describes the path of mankind from an era of knowledge to an era of storytelling, dreams and fantasies: "*The companies of the future will be selling emotions.*" The time of standardised, cheaply and effectively produced articles is out, once we enter the phase of dream society. The markets turn to offering items like adventures, togetherness, friendship and love, caring, who-am-I?-identities, peace of mind or an attractive selection of ideologies.

No wonder, then, that the architects have to read the signs of the time and find their own way of interpreting its spirit. The most visible sign has already been for many years in the lip-service of the market economy. And now, to revisit our particular herd of the wooden horses of architecture, I come to my point. Architecture is harnessed to lend an appealing skin to commercial undertakings of different kinds. It has become a medium for selling the unreality of real estate, the invisibility of transparency, the crumbling solidity, the political slogan of sustainable development to tranquillize our professional consciences, the gestures of mock-ecology to hide the built-in conflicts, to attract public attention to some showpieces of aesthetically motivated follies, *et cetera.*

And why all that? Because this is a storytellers' world. Architecture is mainly asked for as a cover, a mask, a sign. Somewhere behind this bodybuilding lie the real problems. We have only to look at the daily news. "*We're not at home in language. We're at home at home.*"[4]

[3] Rolf Jensen, *Dream Society*, New York, McGraw Hill, 2001.
[4] Daniel Libeskind, "Where are we now ?"(*Architectural Record*, 3/2003)

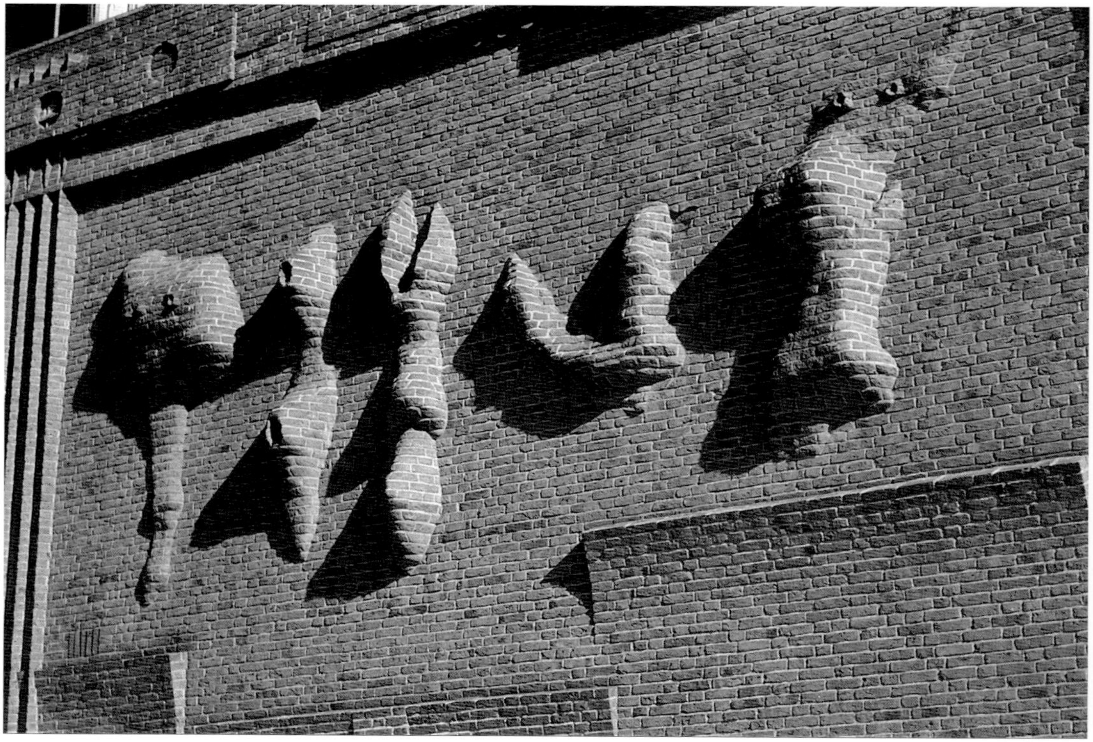

ATTILA'S HORSE

Malcolm Quantrill – Matti K. Mäkinen

Dear Mattikoo,

I don't know who said what, but I really must take issue with your linking the ephemeral world of the butterfly to the role of vernacular architecture. Surely the vernacular qualifies for the status of a baby elephant at least?

I think of the youthful Hilding Ekelund and Alvar Aalto seeking the eternal truth of *architettura minore,* a "lesser architecture", in Tuscany in the 1920s. Those young Finnish architects were looking for evidence of material permanence, which *architettura minore* came to represent in inquisitive minds. This is why Italians also refer to *architettura minore* as *architettura colonica,* because its generic, styleless forms literally colonise the landscape. *Architettura colonica* is not an ephemeral state of affairs, it occupies the terrain, possessing it for Man's fundamental right of settlement, his "rite of dwelling".

Whether we call it *architettura minore*, or more accurately *architettura colonica,* it represents a "permanent determinant" which, because of its colonising characteristics, draws Man's mark upon the land, giving form and direction to his labour. We are not dealing here with some ephemeral fluttering in the wind, but quiet, almost silent statements that shape our perception of farming and agricultural exploration. We better believe that this *architettura colonica* is the Real Stuff!

I can think of other aspects of our architectural world for which the butterfly might serve as a metaphor, but not just now.

With my thanks for the stimulus,
Vuestro sempre, Malcolmo

Dear Malcolm,

Maybe Roger Connah guessed that we are bound to reach this degree of misinterpretation, as he warned me against excessive use of metaphors. And here we are now.

I wrote: *This theme leads us back to the role of architecture vs. mere building. If the monuments are the elephants of architecture, meant to carry their memories over centuries, so the vernacular building might be the dancing butterflies, coming and going, living their day and forgotten tomorrow, replaced by new generations.*

I also assumed that the butterfly's memory is genetically deposited and reappears with the ever renewing generations. This brings back the memory of a sunny day on the Hungarian puszta, where we strolled around flying kites, Imre Makovecz and myself. Makovecz is known for his philosophizing mind, which creates a steady growing ground for his architecture. As we stopped for a rest and sat down in the grass, he ran his fingers through the grass and spoke: "Can you imagine that Attila's horse has trampled on this same grass…new straws every summer and yet…the same grass." Imre went on talking, sinking deeper and deeper into a kind of cosmogony typical for his way of thinking. I lay down on the grass, let my head rest and lowered my ear down. Did I hear the rumble of horse-hoofs shake the ground or was it just a jet flying by somewhere high up? How could I know? Perhaps it was a ghostly image of the past, a wild horde on horseback hurrying to loot and kill, swinging their swords.

Mircea Eliade, writing of the myth of eternal return[1] and the rebirth of time, refers among other themes to the archetypal rituals connected to building. Every time a new house is built , a "new era" is born. All building is an absolutely new beginning. In other words, it is an attempt to bring us back to zero, a total moment without any trace of "history". Building is reorganising the world and life itself. And the myths and rites of building – how profane they ever might appear through the drunken mist of a roof-topping party – maintain more or less the same ancient idea.

This said, I'll return to my dear butterflies, and the basic element of all houses, the vernacular. Maybe this little story of Attila's horse is enough to make my point. While the long-lived Elephant of Architecture still goes strong, the vernacular butterflies appear and disappear, as individuals they live their day and dance their *Totentanz*, but collectively, their generic roots guarantee their eternal return – as far as anything is eternal. And referring to this does not mean any pejorative attitude towards the vernacular base-matter of buildings. On the contrary, I try to accentuate the absolute

[1] Free quotation of Mircea Eliade, *Le Mythe De L'Éternel Retour*, 1949.

importance of this more or less anonymous stock of building, which has provided a warm home for the great majority of mankind. And so it will be, in spite of all missionaries submitting the gospel of architecture.

Mircea Eliade takes up the meaning of history, the individuality and the historicity. Belief in the uniqueness of history and "novelties" is a new invention in the history of mankind. The archaic man was more conservative and defensive against novelties and non-repeatable phenomena.

Actually the span between the wisest Elephant and the least worthwhile Butterfly would deserve some closer study, especially as the gap between the most luxurious palaces and the servants' huts has been filled with buildings, which are not really categorized as this or that. We can ask, if we have a few levels of more or less esteemed Architecture at the highest end of the ladder and the "architecture without architects" on the lower rungs, how can we define the growing amount of material ranking in the higher or lower middle of the scale?

I don't know. The selected examples of architectural publicity seem to concentrate on either ends but who is interested in the average, the mediocre, the customary, the standard, whatever names you can give it? The normal doesn't make headlines, nor does it give birth to heroes. But it makes townscapes, it provides context and background for this Elephant called Architecture.

We can give names, of course. The modern development has brought along a growing stock of commercial buildings where high class architecture has not necessarily been the innermost dream of the investors. The same can be stated of the greatest part of housing, governmental offices, hospitals, schools and even universities. Where the intentions have been aimed at qualities other than high architecture, there the miracle has seldom had a chance. And if the client was ambitious, the architect was not competent enough to use the chance offered. And so we have been able to develop a remarkable amount of some slimy mass I would call *neovernacular* – middle-class at its best. *Semitecture* could be a title as well, to avoid casting an undeserved shadow on the authentic vernacular 'folk architecture'.

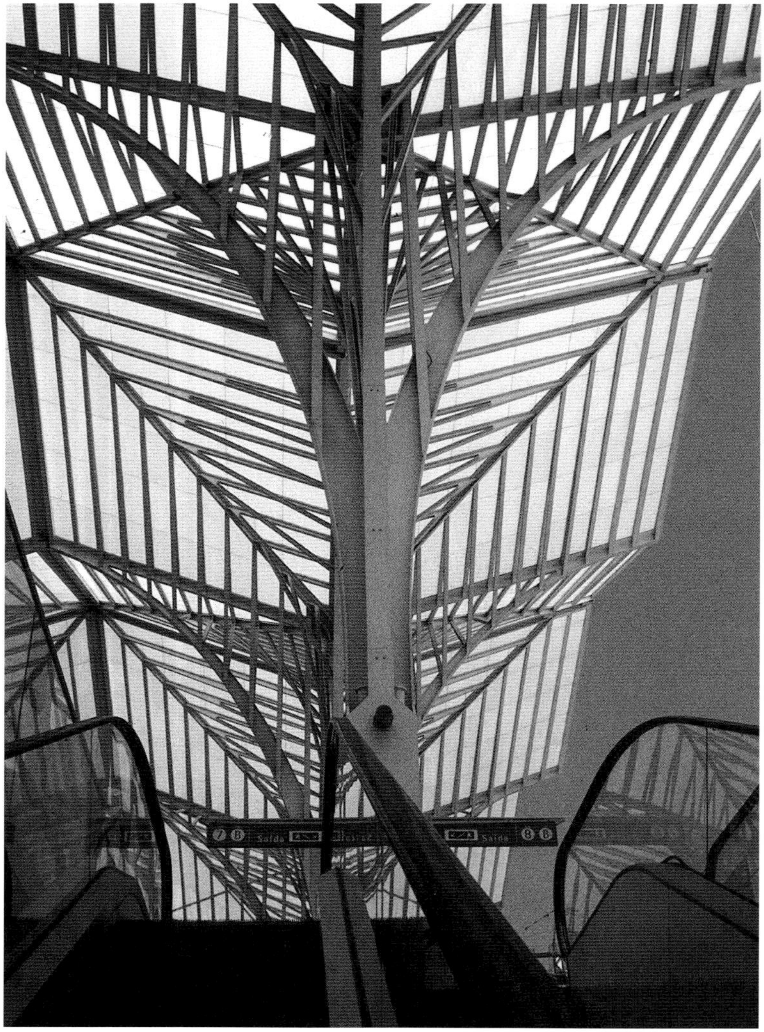
Saida
Saida

WOODEN HORSE OR DANCING ELEPHANT

Malcolm Quantrill

I'd like to return to the questions[1] *raised concerning the pairing of the "Elephant" with the "Butterfly" in approaching architecture and architectural theory.*

We have already reviewed the contrast of the Elephant's "weight, substance and durability" (Vitruvius's "Commoditas" and "Firmitas", if not "Venustas"!) against the "weightlessness, ephemerality and luminescence" (which might represent the character and image of more recent glass architecture) of the Butterfly. In addition, I drew attention to the strange phenomenon present in the third movement of Robert Schumann's piano studies, *Papillons* [Butterflies] of 1829–31, which exhibits a markedly clumsy, unbutterflyish, and discordant ponderousness.

This sudden change of mood may be explained NOT by Schumann's adherence to a programmatic outline based on some nature study or butterfly imagery, but rather depends on more eclectic sources drawn from and inspired by J.P.F. Richter's novel, *Flegeljahre* ["Awkward Age"]. In fact, Schumann told his family that *Papillons* was intended as a musical representation of the novel's *Larventanz* or "masked ball". Indeed, he went so far as to mark in his copy of Richter's novel those passages that correspond to the first ten of the twelve short movements which make up *Papillons.*

Thus, by highlighting the text Schumann wanted us to believe that the third movement of *Papillons* was inspired by this passage: "He was attracted to and astonished most of all by a giant boot that was sliding around the floor dressed in itself". Despite Schumann's disclaimer that he had "fitted the words to the music and not vice versa", the intrusive influence of that giant boot is all too evident in the weighty cadence of the third movement of *Papillons.*

So, let us recapitulate the progress of our analogies so far. We are confronted first of all by the Elephant, which clearly stands for the maintenance of traditional solidity in architecture, a condition more or less maintained until the middle of the nineteenth century. But at that point, Paxton's Crystal Palace began to convey the "weightlessness, ephemerality and luminescence", namely the

[1] Kristian Gullichsen

"Butterfly", of a new architecture. Thus, our architecture today can be seen as having been freed from the primeval forests of an "Elephant Era", occupying instead an open landscape that allows and promotes cross-cultural pollination.

Meanwhile, what about the architect? How have his anatomy and psyche been affected in this progress from "substance" to "luminescence"? At this point Russian avant-garde composer Igor Stravinsky enters on stage. Stravinsky was 60 years old in 1942, but he was still as full of beans as he had been in the 1920s. To attest to this continuing virility he knocked off a little dance number, a mere four minutes worth of music, with the provocative title of *Circus Polka for a Baby Elephant.*

And there we have it, as the Emperor summarizes in the film *Amadeus.* Today our architect can begin to practice new steps, no longer a substantial heavyweight "jumbo", but a mere babe of the new age. Now he practices his polka in tune with its appropriate uncertainty of cadence, venturing out into a landscape of unknown delights. And he may do so in the confidence that, as with Stravinsky's "Baby Elephant", the choreography of his dance routine will mature eventually into a symbiosis of symbolic forms.

4

HEROES AND STATUES

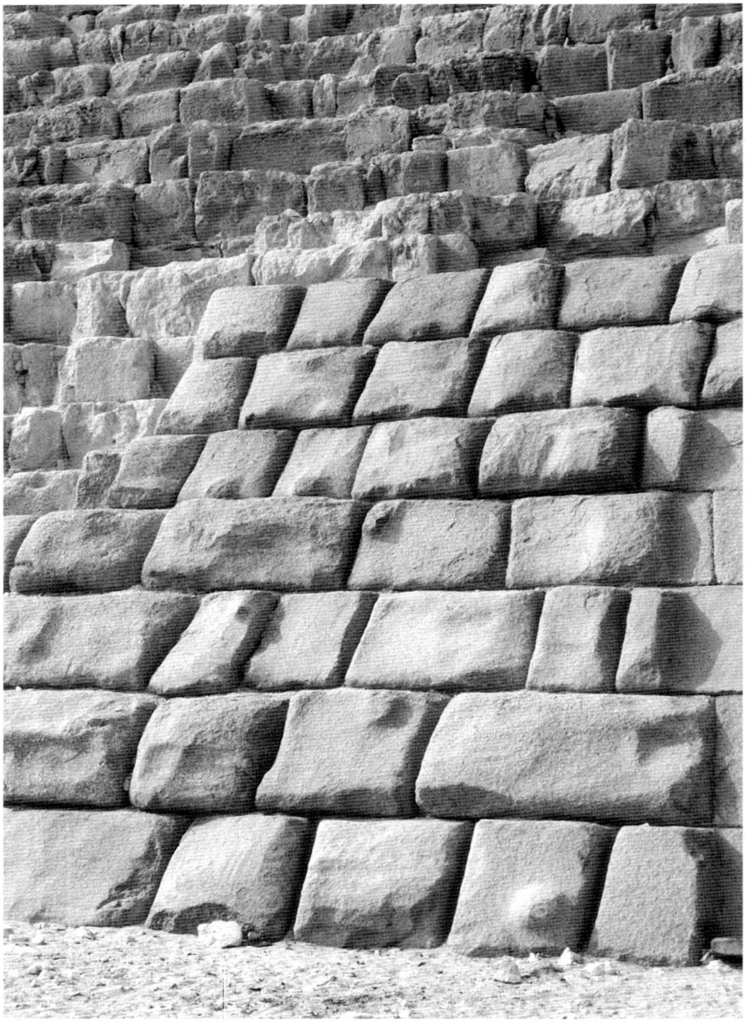

GROWING OFF SCALE

Matti K. Mäkinen

Big is beautiful. Shall we make it
big or colossal or monumental?

Dear Malcolm,

You open up the question of scale on American soil. And why not, in many aspects the US stands as a symbol of bigness. In America everything is big, from blueberries to hamburgers, all the way up to the buldings scratching the navel of the skies. This carnal push symbolises simultaneously the skyward trend of thought.[1] Up, higher, faster, closer to God. Love of the Big, a Babylon tower syndrome? Or the Colossus of Rhodes? Or the Soviet Union? Something within the field of social psychology? Or the market economy? Or whatever? Until the biggest of them crashes. "God bless America", as the President of the United States customarily ends his speeches.

In these secular times, it is interesting to see and hear how important this Celestial Patron is for the Americans. Even the worst losers and non-believers, if they get hold of a dollar bill, can fold it up and be comforted by the "In God We Trust" printed on every goddam note. To most Europeans making money has traditionally been a suspicious activity, which the Americans have pursued beyond the acceptable limits of decency. But if we listen to the voice of America, Americans are only enjoying the good American life. And that's what they feel entitled to: a promised land of health and riches, even beauty and happiness. "God Bless You, America".

I have a sense of hesitation, when I mention the Ground Zero. Who am I, sitting safely – as I naively believe – in this remote Finland. Here I sat at my TV two years ago and listened to the echo of the big bang that made the very foundations of good American life tremble? Yet this case of the former twin towers has so much to do with my topic here, with the phenomenon called architecture, with the upwards surge of man's nest-building. Why do I hesitate? Manhattan lives within a stream of environmental change, buildings going frequently up and down. But this blasting catastrophe

[1] Quoted from the title of Thomas A.P. van Leeuwen, *The Skyward Trend of Thought,* The Metaphysics of the American Skyscraper, MIT Press, Cambridge, Mass., 1986.

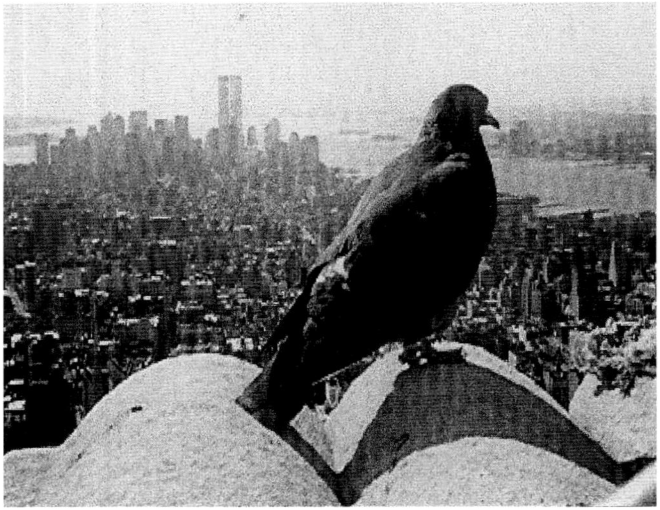

brought along such a massive burden of human tragedy and suffering that even touching the case as one of purely architectural and urban planning matters feels delicate.

In an earlier letter, I have already mentioned how in 1960, on my first occasion in New York, I admired the clean-cut appearance of the Seagram Building, as it stood out against a background made of 19th century towers. A gem that astonishingly soon was to lose its individual shine, melting into the new developments of neighboring glass boxes. Anyway, the Empire State Building could not lose its noble dominance, its slender body ruling the scenery with a self-explanatory ease – until the twin towers appeared, an unexpected feat in an unexpected location, deforming the natural shape of the Manhattan skyline, pressing down the edge of Manhattan shore with their massive weight. As an architect, I just could not understand why; why they had to be built in that form. And why did I not notice any local criticism? Anyway, it was none of my business. I was a foreigner. Maybe I just don't understand some higher meaning, or some higher way of building, I thought. Maybe this was only a beginning, outbalancing some still higher development that was being prepared somewhere on somebody's drafting board.

As the ruins of the Twin Towers were cleared, the future of the location was under study. As Daniel Libeskind presented his winning scheme for rebuilding, I agreed with many others that here might be a compromise between the real estate interests and the townscape values. Even the tragic history seemed to have its symbolic expressions in the painful wreathing of the lower masses and, of course, a victorious gesture of crowning the scheme with a needlepoint tower could be understood as nearly a necessity, even psychologically.

The story continues in a way that could be foreseen. At the moment of writing this, the developer has already had his say; the architect and his ideas have been moved to one side, while the tower seems to remain as high as ever, though it has lost its needle-like shape. And, as expected, the violent forms of the lower parts of the complex have given way to more normalised office space. The way the situation seems now is that Daniel Libeskind was used as a jockey, galloping to win the race on a richly decorated mare, but who in a later study was unmasked and became a Trojan horse.

Michael Sorkin comments on the latest development in the New York scenery, including the Ground Zero process, as follows:

"The core of the ethical performance of a building lies in its program, and we must take responsibility for a building's behavior as well as its artistic presence. Indeed, "good design" is often a cover for the ethically questionable; witness the old saw, 'If you want to build a bad building, hire a good architect. And if you want to build an outrageous building, hire a distinguished architect': The most outstanding instance of this tactic is, of course, Ground Zero, where 'distinguished' architecture has been used to con the public into supporting a massive office scheme. But there are other examples, as well. Suddenly, after years of disheartening indifference, the city is awash with proposals by global star architects, and a clear majority seem to be involved in leveraging projects of dubious ethical provenance." [2]

Bigness is a product of growth. Whatever, whoever, wherever you are, you start out with a small beginning. The growth takes you, surges you along on a gliding scale – *glissando* goes the melody of your advance.

"Bigness is inescapable. Since the beginning of the Industrial Revolution, civilization has been inexorably set on a course to increasing size. Cities become ever larger and more land-hungry; transport systems become more capacious; corporations have to become bigger and bigger so they can compete with a hope of success in the global market." [3]

Architecture, as a mirror reflecting the prevailing values, has naturally been adjusted to the actual concepts of size, proportion and scale. It has accepted, adopted and even exaggerated the physical dimensions of its products, or should I say achievements. Tall, that is the tower. Since time beyond memory has long meant some form of shed. And large, that is the town on its way to becoming the core of a metropolis, or one of the cores of a bigger metropolis. Bigness is often interpreted as a sign of greatness. Great architects are commissioned to design great buildings for great rulers. And the easiest way to make greatness visible is to give it a big, exaggerated appearance.

Those architects who cannot find their way close enough to the ruling circles can seek their luck in propagating the human scale. I sincerely believe that all the talk and all the writings about the idea of human scale are not only another way to success by a populist approach. I believe that this warming issue of humanism, the human, the humane, close to the needs of the little man, can also be genuine.

Okay, we have good will. But then come the questions, and even doubt can emerge. A human scale, easily referred to, but what precisely does it mean?

Is it possible that the emotional contact with the human scale starts in the womb? Is it possible that somewhere in a mental pocket of ancient memory we carry a sensation of a nest, its size, its warm intimacy, the softness of the wall close to your body? If this is your personal – and simultaneously prehistorical – starting point, then the only direction for further development is that of growth.

[2] Michael Sorkin: "When good architects design bad buildings: Beauty trumps ethics", *Architectural Record*, 08/2004. Sorkin is the director of the graduate urban design program at City College of New York.
[3] Peter Davey, Comment in *The Architectural Review*, August 2002

You grow out of the womb, you fly out of the nest, you move out of the parents' house, out of your home town. You grow, your dreams unfold, the scale of your impact on your surroundings finds its measures.

Our life world is extended to new dimensions outside the limits of direct perception. Child psychologist Jean Piaget sums up his investigations with the statement, that our perception of space involves a gradual construction "and certainly does not exist ready-made at the outset of mental development".[4] Christian Norberg-Schulz makes a list of five different space concepts: the *pragmatic* space of physical action, the *perceptual* space of immediate orientation, the *existential* space which forms Man's stable image of his environment, the *cognitive* space of the physical world, and, finally, the *abstract* space of pure logical relations.[5]

I allow my mind to glide up and down this range of spaces. At the lower end I find my own physical dimension, a haptic space, where I only stretch out my hands and my feet, and feel around. Maybe this is the dimension of an imagined nest. Imagined, because a human's nest – if such a thing ever existed – must have been dimensioned for some size of a family, not for single individuals. Further up the list I find the existential space. That must be my daily sphere of living, moving and acting, this is Metropolitan Helsinki. The cognitive space…hmm-h, places I have visited but not daily, Paris or Mexico, I don't see them but I know they are there. And then within the cognitive sphere I can also include places which I never visited but for sure, they are there, like Antarctis or the Moon.

My literary source dates from 1971. The computer era was comparatively young at that time. The new spaces, derived as the path of abstract spaces of logical thinking was extended, could not be seen at that time. Now we could continue the list and include the "*virtual* space", spaces produced by computer technology. I can take a virtual space, created by CAD, perceive it, observe it from varying distances, take a look from different angles, change the colours if I feel like… Is this kind of phenomenon real? A philosophical question, I assume. Anyway, there it is, in the middle of my perceptional space. – Norberg-Schulz mentioned also an *expressive or artistic* space. Maybe these computerised spaces could belong to that group, with an observation on the side that many, maybe most, of them are not created to serve artistic intentions, including even all of those conjured on their screens by architects.

Charles Jencks, in a letter to the editor of *The Architectural Review* comments: "Man is not the measure of all things, nor is the universe as a whole – but rather, as the new paradigm scientist Ilya Prigogine said, the continual dialogue between the two."[6]

[4] Jean Piaget and Bärbel Inhelder, *The Child's Conception of Space*, W.W. Norton and Co, New York, 1956
[5] Christian Norberg-Schulz, *Existence, Space & Architecture*, Praeger, New York, 1971
[6] Charles Jencks, in "Views", *The Architectural Review*, August 2003

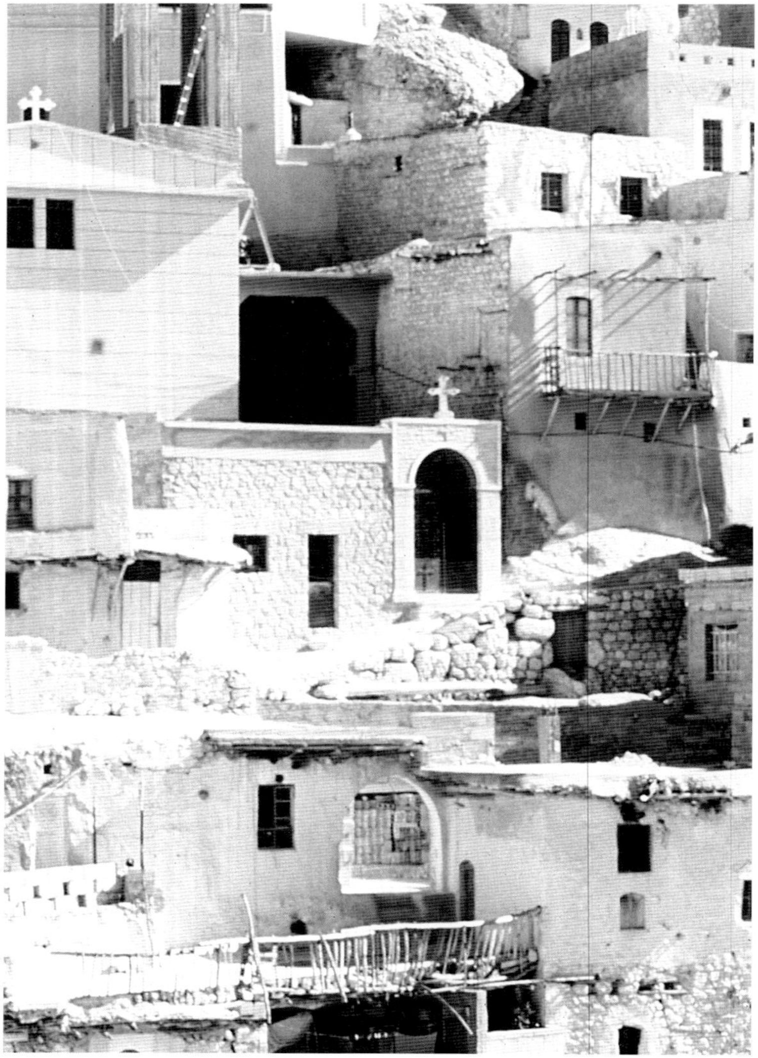

OF HUMAN SCALE

Matti K. Mäkinen

Everything is best when it is
tempered to its own importance.
Leon Battista Alberti

A strict principle of Alberti's typology of buildings[1] is that what is appropriate for rulers is not necessarily appropriate for private persons. *Quod licet Jovi, non licet bovi.* What is appropriate in the case of a queen is not appropriate in the case of a courtesan, for instance, even if she were a famous one: "I would not criticize Artemis, queen of Carla, for building her beloved and noble husband a most magnificent tomb", Alberti remarks, but he cannot approve "of that famous harlot, Rhodope of Thrace, who had a tomb constructed for herself at vast expense, for although her immoral earnings had left her the wealth of a queen, in no way did she deserve a tomb fit for one."

The kings and queens in Alberti's *De Re aedificatoria* are allowed to carry out almost superhuman projects. "Let them join sea to sea by cutting through intervening land; let them level mountains and valleys; let them create new islands, and again join existing ones to the mainland; let them leave behind feats that could never be imitated, and in so doing preserve their name for posterity."

In some ancient cultures, rulers were gods, or at least demi-gods, delegates of some Holy Divinity. This sacred capacity was inherited over generations by the Royal Houses. In the next step down the ladder of history, the Kingdom was supported by the Constitution. Then comes the era of Democracy, and the new rulers are elected by Parties who elect their delegates who will in turn be elected by the citizens to represent all the People. And now, the highest throne has been given to the Economy, whose leading forces are elected by the decisions of the investors.

Of course, this is quite a shortcut through the political history of the world. The only justification is my eagerness to return closer to my competence. Now I jump out of the train of history and

[1] Leon Battista Alberti, *De Re aedificatoria* (1485), as interpreted in Liisa Kanerva's PhD dissertation *Defining the Architect in Fifteenth Century Italy*, Helsinki, Tiedekirja, 1998.

continue my study of the visible and invisible hands holding the strings with which to manipulate the contemporary architect.

Architects have always preferred to work in close contact with rulers and the ruling classes. Thus, the dream clients today are the superpowers of the economy, the worldwide corporations and their top managers. If the task of architecture – and thus the *raison d´etre* of the architects – was to serve the Kings and Queens in erecting the physical symbols of power and wealth, they are now serving the organisations of the global and local market economy for similar purposes. Of course, the real idea of modern construction carries the messages in a more refined way. Now the key issues centre on persuasion rather than force, advertising instead of commanding, giving the impression of transparency instead of keeping hold of important secrets. A steady job is a price, not a punishment, and work must be experienced as a privilege, as fun, enjoyment of freedom, an admittance to good company, membership of a happy family. The unhappy family you can leave behind at home. All these delights demand one condition: you have to perform in a favorable proportion, not only to cover your salary but also to meet the needs of your employer, and more especially the investors behind him.

This way of thought leads us to the symbolism of the tower and shed. The architects dedicated and privileged to design the towers live in the hope of getting their share of the crumbs from the name and fame their tower patrons are craving for. In spite of the standardised allowance of creativity in tayloring the business uniform for a building, some dreams of the architects do come true. One common denominator is the sheer size of the object. If you design the highest building in the world, you are Somebody, at least until the next tower overshadows yours.

We stated already how America is the cradle of Bigness. In Finland, we have to find other ways if we wish to be Something. Here, the search for a human scale has been a repeatedly occuring phrase for those with the power to occupy the tower. The more power, the higher you sit in the tower. The tower is simultaneously one of the oldest and strongest symbols of man's built environment, easily readable, a highly masculine scent hovering around its phallistics. Just have a look at the Swiss Re "gherkin", one of the newest eyesores in the London cityscape. And everywhere these towers provide "day-care" homes for those executing the so-called intellectual work, which replaced the earlier drudgery of clerks. The rapid pace of the modernisation and accordingly the urbanisation of both the country and the minds of its people has rolled as a *tsunami-wave* over the agrarian society.

In the Albertian city "a house like its owner, should be a good citizen". The idea of a city in which the social structure of the community is expressed in buildings with such a precision as Alberti advocates is a fascinating one. A system which makes it possible to construct a city as an architectural entity, in which every detail can be read as a sign revealing the inhabitant's place in the social hierarchy offers a real architectural language. Such an interpretation of architecture was certainly natural to Alberti the orator, whose main interest, after all, was in language.[2]

Finns are lonely riders and so are Finnish architects. A great part of the renown of Finnish architecture consists of buildings located distinctly apart from their environment. Our architecture – as soon as it was called architecture – was never created to fill a gap within a wall-to-wall urban structure. Yet our old wooden towns from the 18th and 19th centuries followed strictly the orthogonally regulated planning ideology of their time. As a good part of them were replaced with multistorey blocks of flats in the latter half of the 20th century, you could say good-bye to a strong tradition in our urban culture. It was not only a matter of built environment. The social structures as well as the cultivated layers of urban manners were shattered simultaneously. I wonder if Finland was the only place where such a loss of memory can be so clearly registered?

In a future-oriented time – perhaps we can give this definition to our own period – the past is not the problem. The problem is what to do now, and how to do it better than our grandparents. In the accelerating stream of global exchange, capital, people, ideas and ideologies, we wish to keep the Finnish trademark – or benchmark. We wish to keep and develop our own melting pot for the influences of American technology and Russian sentiment, while maintaining our own identity, even in the fields of urban planning and architecture. Small in size, big in dreams: could this characterise our idea of a happy future? And would it, in turn, offer a human scale for planning?

[2] Ibid.

THE PRIMA MATERIA OF ARCHITECTURE

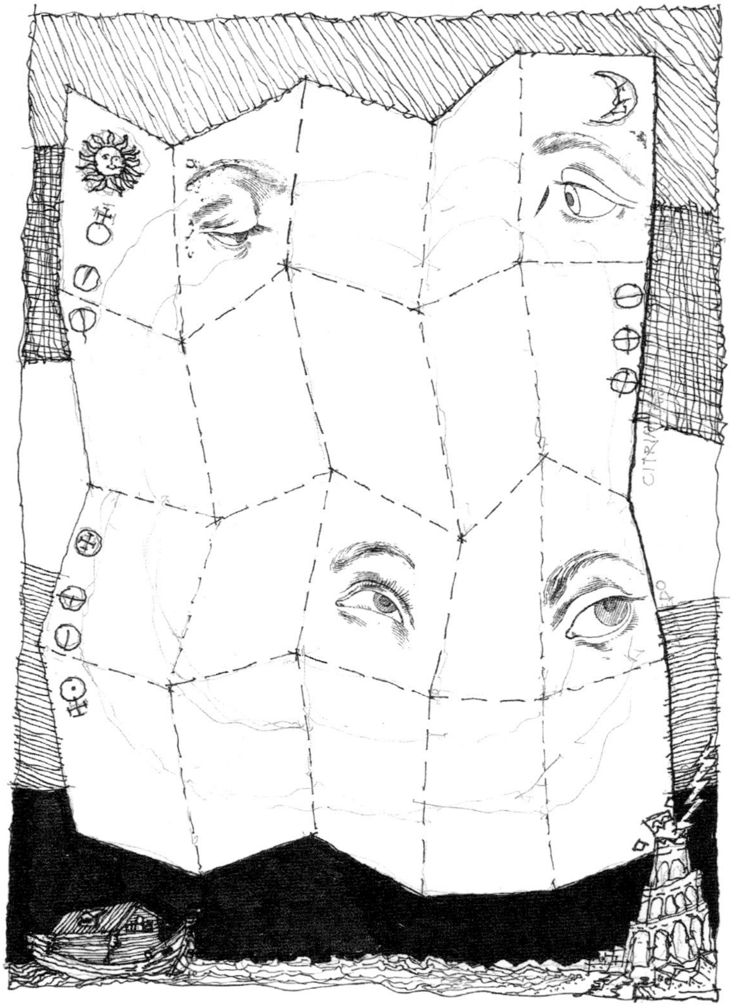

HEROIC SHAMANISM

Matti K. Mäkinen

– What is the difference between an architect and a building contractor?
– The builder knows everything but doesn't understand anything, the architect understands everything but doesn't know anything.
– And what about the structural engineer, then?
– He *doesn't know that he doesn't understand anything.*

You might call this a kind of shamanism. In architecture, the most famous Shamans have been in Finland, Reima Pietilä; and in Hungary, Imre Makovecz.

As the 1992 World Expo was to be located in Seville, Spain, many countries organized competitions to find the best architecture for their national pavillions. Reima Pietilä had won the competition for the Finnish pavillion in Brussels 1955, which was a good start for the young Pietilä, just 31 years old. In 1992, the prize-winning project for the Finnish pavillion was designed by a group of 5 young architects. A critic sees in the winning entry some political and architectural significance, comparable to the Finnish Pavillion at Paris 1900, where Eliel Saarinen with his partner Herman Gesellius were the architects. Peter MacKeith writes: "Foreign observers look at Finnish architecture in continuous search for the "next generation" a new modern heroism, a new arctic Shaman, a new northern humanism, a Finnish architecture of silence".[1]

At the Seville Expo, the Hungarian maestro Imre Makovecz may have been overacting in the rural Hungarian Shaman style he had exercised during many years in his native country, but the Finnish Pavillion was quite a success. One way or the other, the modern combination of a slightly curved box with walls of wooden scaling in a natural colour, in juxtaposition with a stern rectangular edifice of steel evoked ideas of mystery. Perhaps a modern Shaman was felt to dwell here, too ? Yes indeed, but where?

[1] Peter MacKeith, "Finland and Finnish Architecture in Seville", *Arkkitehti/Finnish Architectural Review*, 4–5/1992

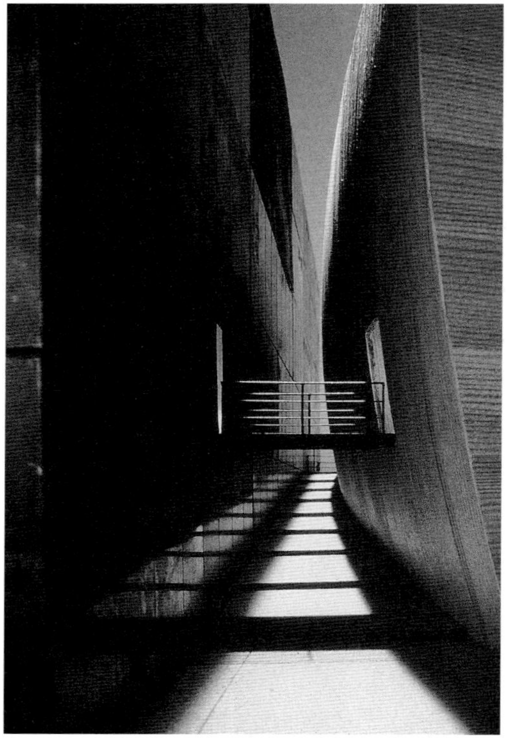

In the early '90s a Shaman spirit was hovering in the air, at least in the Finnish experience. High up in northern Finland, the architects Heikkinen and Komonen designed the airport terminal at Rovaniemi, where the airfield is located right at the Arctic Circle. Assisted by a conceptual artist, they designed the main hall with an oblong opening in the ceiling and drafted a curved figure on the floor. And then, lo, on a sunny day, you can see how the rays of the northern sun travel along this curve. The analemma of sun, it's called. But this is not the whole story. After some longer period of time, the arctic circle has moved slightly to a new location, and....well, who remembers the story and who can understand the meanings hidden, and who cares? We go on flying, anyway.

But we can fly safely in the conviction that we have met some very significant and important apparition. Besides, we have been touched by the hand of a solar time-piece, we have seen the Ancient in embrace with the Modern. The terminal building has been enriched with a story.. And in this era of story-telling!

But this is not the end of the story. Some months later, I visited Cranbrook, Michigan, and I was standing at the gateway to the Academy compound. And then the Rector of the Academy of Art gives an enthusiastic lecture. What we see in front of us, a small group of foreign visitors, is a composition of some freestanding columns, boldly upright with no load to carry.

But what is important – and so unique in this setting – is that under certain circumstances, the solar Analemma is marked by these columns. This wonderful combination of Art and Philosophy has been designed by the Finnish architect Juhani Pallasmaa.

Admiringly, I looked up and down those pillars, with a distant memory of the *analemma* at Rovaniemi airport, thousands of miles away, conceived by another pair of well-known Finnish architects. It seems that Shamanism knows no boundaries.

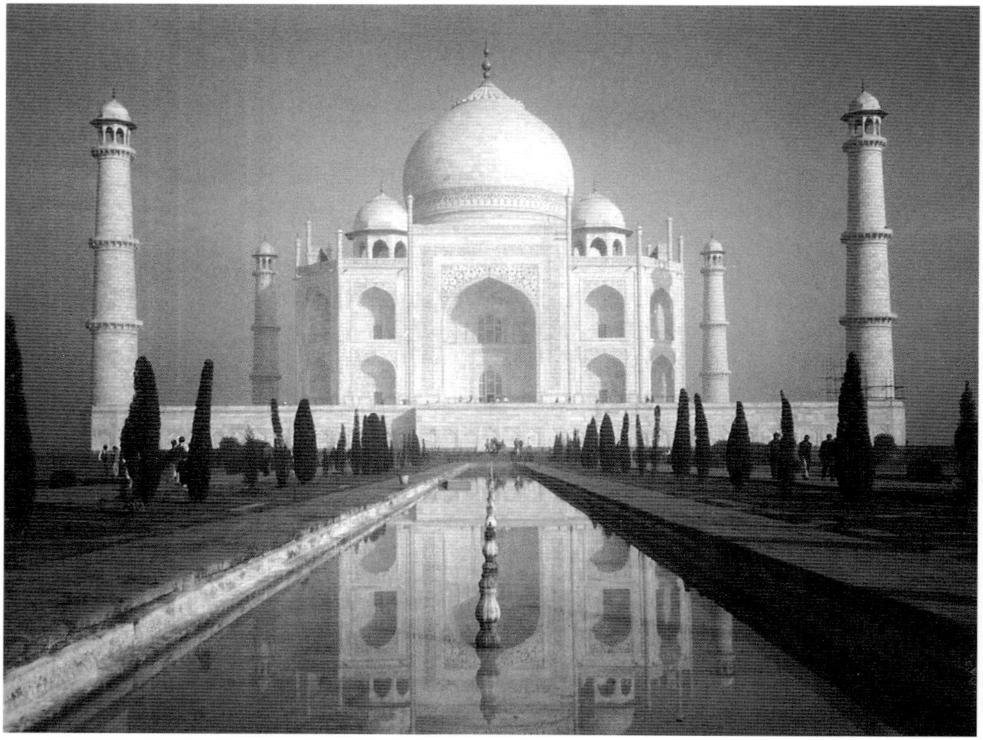

THE FAME IS THE GAME

Matti K. Mäkinen

Throughout history, the remarkable buildings were made to glorify gods, kings, queens, nobles or otherwise "better people".

First come the gods, of course, the sacred places, the sacred buildings, the shrines, temples and cathedrals. Then come the castles, palaces and residences. Later on, descending down the steps, come the administrative buildings to serve the bureaucracies of states and towns, the parliaments, the palaces of law and justice, the town halls, the universities, the residences of knights and bishops, and then come the houses of the high and mighty, the homes of the wealthy bourgoise and the factory patrons. And along with this representative procession marches the architect. Until this point, I avoided mentioning vernacular buildings and the unknown designers, if there were any. And I'll keep this line, because here we are discussing this thing called Architecture. Again, we have to remember that architecture is what the architecture world considers to be architecture.

What is the most beautiful building in the world? Oh, you have heard? The Taj Mahal, of course! Or is it still topping the list? But who was the architect? You don't know? Let's see.

For a long time, the Taj Mahal in India has been praised as the most beautiful piece of architecture. According to several sources, the temple was built by *Architect* Emperor Shah Jahan in the memory of his dear wife and queen Mumtaz Mahal at Agra, India. It is an "elegy in marble" or some say an expression of a dream. The Taj Mahal was constructed over a period of twenty-two years, employing twenty thousand workers and muslim craftsmen, and was completed in 1648. The construction documents show that its master architect was Ustad 'Isa, the renowned Islamic architect of his time.

The first architect known by name was the Egyptian Imhotep, from the era of the pyramids. For a long time after him, most architects had to remain in the all-embracing shadows of their royal clients, so that in the media of these millennia the news told of how, say, "The Emperor Soandso built this remarkable monument". On the other hand, this custom has survived until our day, where especially the lesser architects are often forgotten in the advertising machinery, tuned to sing the glory of the patron organisations and their leaders.

There is no need to repeat the history of name and fame in world architecture. The history of architecture, with and without names, was written more or less within the sphere of the western civilisation. Architecture as it was taught in the years when I studied was not a product of the colonised continents. Thus, for instance, Indian architecture started with Le Corbusier, his personal achievements in Chandigarh and his wide influence. Relatively the same was the case with South America, with Costa and Niemayer in Brasil. The architecture of the colonies consisted of replicas of European churches, banks and palaces, following the Spanish, Portuguese and British models. Architecture was a beneficial part of "white man's burden" carried overseas.

On the old continent, histories of architecture have been registered, persons named and styles classified since the early times of antiquity. Alberti praises also the anonymous maestros, the builders of ancient Rome:

"There was such an incredible surfeit of talent in this field that at one time, I read, seven hundred architects were being employed in Rome alone, whose work could scarcely be praised enough."

Alberti has also included in *De Re aedificatoria* the architectural deeds of such men of Greek origin as Archimedes, Daedalus, Callimachus, Chersiphron and Methagenes. Their names nowadays have rather the ring of a myth, but from the fifteenth-century point of view their contribution to architecture appeared real and undeniable. They were considered as representatives of the glorious early phase of the art of building.[1]

At this point, I span a bridge over some five centuries and arrive to our own era.

Something in the spirit of architectural education leads to a competitive atmosphere, where the intentions are directed from the *good* to the *better*. Better than the others. Doing better than the others and making the others realise and admit it. I am The Architect, who are you? Schopenhauer writes of the three ways of evaluating a person: What you are, what you have and what the others think you are. Being, having and – I was about to write loving – but, with a second thought, dropped it. Pretending to be, looking like, giving the impression of being somebody, that's what I mean.

You have to be famous to get commissions. You have to get commissions to be famous. This is the name of the publicity game. Our time is the era of heroes – and heroines. The publicity needs heroes. The public needs heroes. Mankind needs heroes – or does it? What makes a hero? Checking the most visible heroes, you have different ways to reach the throne. You look good. Or you sound good. Or

[1] Liisa Kanerva, *Defining the Architect in Fifteenth Century Italy*, The Finnish Academy of Science and Letters, Helsinki, 1998. In her doctoral thesis-based book, Kanerva concentrates on *De Re aedifatoria* and exemplary architects discussed by Leon Battista Alberti.

you are incredibly promiscuous. Or you have astounding legs. Or you are the second richest person in the world. Or the publicity has found you because you are the absolute Nobody.

To be Anybodies we need Nobodies. Would there be only one colour, there would be no colour at all. If nobody wants to play the part of Nobody, we have to create one, maybe by arranging a contest for electing the Mister/Miss Mundane Nobody. A critical look at the contemporary publicity might reveal that these contests are already arranged, only under a different heading. As a matter of fact, the architectural profession is crowded with nobodies. In the architectural world, you can be a most acceptable person with a hyper-decent lifestyle. You can be a good father and a faithful husband, patriotic, middle-income, kind to the neighbours' dog and to the old lady crossing the street. Professionally, you can design buildings that the owners adore – homely, nice, fitting into the scenery. No go. To the architectural publicity this does not sell. These capacities never make a hero. Something else is needed. And what could this something be?

You must be news. Whatever – it is not so important. But relax: Fame comes or goes, all that is needed is Luck. And how to find the keys is outside logical calculation. But so is Architecture, as well.

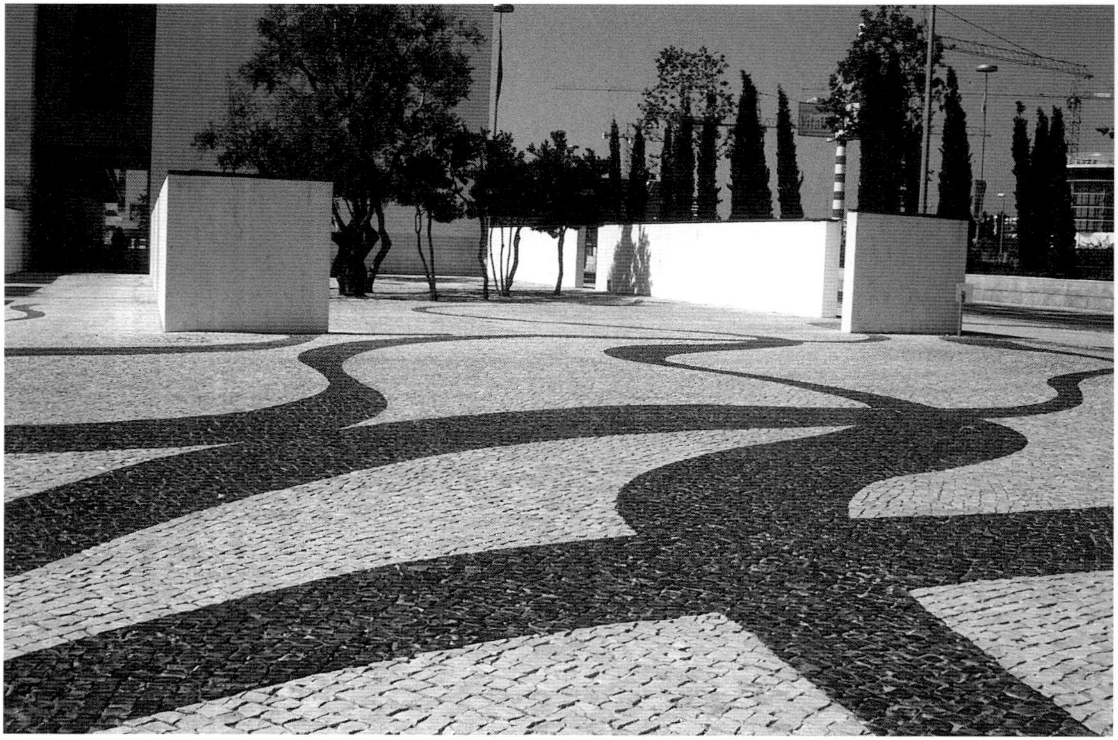

FAKE, IMITATION OR PRETEND ARCHITECTURE

Malcolm Quantrill

My dear Mattikoo,

I live in Texas, in the suburb of a major American State University. Notice that I do NOT say in the shadow of that university! This is because the university in question has no "Body of Architecture" to generate the casting of such a shadow. In fact, the buildings that merit the status of Architecture may be counted on the fingers of one hand. Actually, there are only three such buildings. The first two are designed in the Romantic Classic tradition, while the third represents a genuine attempt to embrace the principles of Modernism.

Perhaps this apparent scarcity of architecture on a university campus poses a fundamental problem? How can the component parts of "The Body of Knowledge", what we commonly call WISDOM, be properly housed if there are literally not enough pieces of architecture to go round? If a university sufficiently values and honours its collective Body of Knowledge, surely it must want to guarantee that it is housed appropriately and with dignity. Unfortunately, the answer seems to be: "Apparently not". Furthermore, it is now quite common for those universities suffering architectural impoverishment to enter into a form of argument known as "special pleading".

A prime example of this attitude goes something like this: *In times of economic distress it is not always possible to afford the cost of True Architecture, so we are frequently compelled instead to make do with Fake – with some sort of imitation Architecture.* Neither Benedictine nor Cistercian abbots would have dared report such a shortfall to their God. But modern Deans of Chapter are more tutored in money matters than either ethics or aesthetics. They may be good at raising funds but, by and large, they have neither the interest in, nor knowledge of, raising edifices worthy of their patrons. In this state of ignorance, they conceal the true facts within their special pleading. Allow me to explain.

As the *quattrocento* came to an end, Domenico Morosini, a Venetian procurator set down his principles for the ordering of cities. His book *de bene instituta* established the prerequisites for architectural dignity and magnificence, which apply as much to the design of a university campus as to a city. Morosini defines the task:

"The art of architecture, of building walls, of woodwork, ironwork, stonework are necessary arts that promote the greater increase of a city's scale and beauty. It is therefore right for a well-governed institution to employ experienced architects rather than untrained or rough ones."

And he goes on to emphasize that:

"It is possible to build something well or badly for the same amount, and that which is well-built will be praised by the citizens, while that which is poorly built must be rejected and cursed."

While Morosini decreed "all civic buildings should be suitably embellished" and the streets connecting them "laid out in an orderly fashion" (an expression of his undisguised contempt for the maze-like patterns of medieval thoroughfares!), he stressed that "principal public buildings should be made splendid". In addition, in order to safeguard the achievement and maintenance of these new standards in the design of cities, Morosini proposed the establishment of an administration for controlling the city's image and adornment – "ad ornatum civitatis".

Those administrators who rake in money for the so-called embellishment of a university campus commonly disburse those funds to pay for poorly conceived and badly constructed academic buildings. Such facilitators (administrators, unaware) seemingly ignorant of the architectural advice available to them, are (often totally) frequently neglectful of the guidance that can be provided by resort to Morosini's control mechanism of "ad ornatum civitatis". In consequence these would-be academic leaders are commonly guilty of spending development funds on Fake or "Pretend Architecture" instead of investing it wisely in the posterity of the "real stuff". And when people ask me how to tell the "pretend stuff" from the "real stuff", I tell them: "In its pretentiousness you shall see its falsehood!"

Unfortunately, the scene here in this academic community is even worse than that! "Fake architecture" is a virulent disease of the region. Encouraged by the University's bad example, developers have rushed in and spread its spores throughout all our new suburbs herein *Collegio Esse*. Especially in Texas the infectious spores and rotting facades of *architettura falsificare* have been fermented to make new limits of hideousness available.

With most of our old housing stock already occupied, it is an affront to our senior professors that they have no alternative but to buy into this junk market. The essential ingredient of this fakery is "a robust pretentiousness", the very pretension conjuring up obvious associations with "pretend architecture". And this disease has spread with equal virulence to create fakery in restaurants, stores, civic buildings and even religious masks!

Saludos cordiales,

Malcolmo.

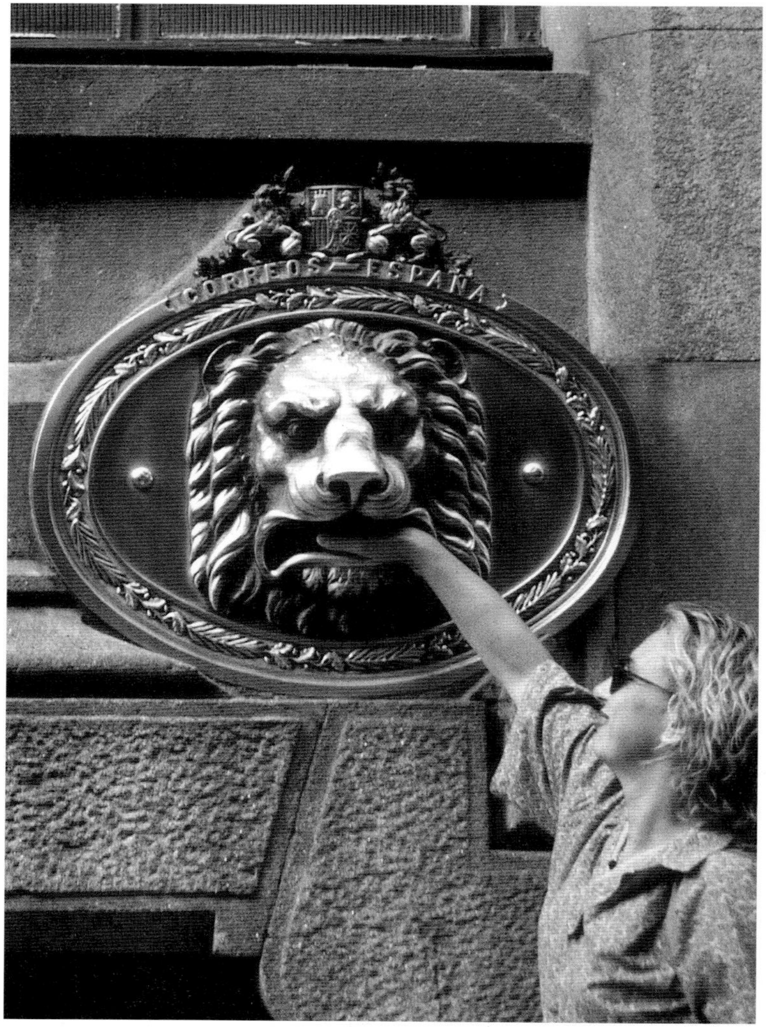
CORREOS — ESPAÑA

THE ART OF TRADING TRADITION

Matti K. Mäkinen – Malcolm Quantrill

Dear Malcolm,

You write, with reference to Peter Brook:

So far, I've discovered two of Brook's viewpoints that might seem relevant to our enquiry: Since theatre is drawn from life, Brook asks how does it differ from life itself? How does its compression of life's experiences work?

How does Shakespeare manage to cram into just 2–3 hours the thoughts and actions of not one but several men and women?

AND *if theatre is quite different from our "normal" lives, what would be the consequence of not having it? In other words: "Is its compression and mirroring of human existence a totally necessary reflection of our being and understanding of that being?"*

Vide "Without architecture where would we be?" To which one is tempted to shout out:

"NOWHERE, *that's* WHERE *we'd be.*"

Let's see, playing the theatre game, acting as another playwright and bringing Architecture on the stage. Isn't architecture also a sort of theatre? According to Karsten Harries: *Architecture is an art of representation.*

What kind of an art is theatre, then?

I make reference to a text dealing with Peter Brook's thinking. Brook himself has said:

"Even if it's ancient, by its very nature theatre is always an art of modernity. A phoenix that has to be constantly brought back to life. Because the image that communicates in the world in which we live, the right effect which creates a direct link between performance and audience, dies very quickly. In five years a production is out of date."

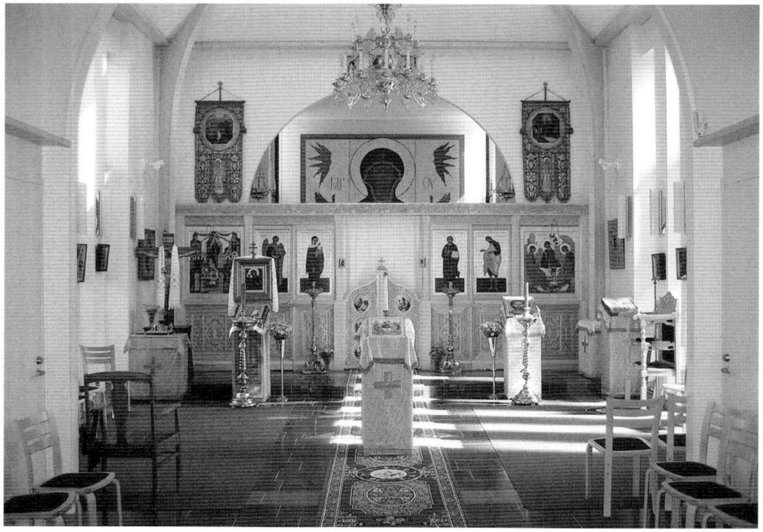

Just for the fun of it, I try to fit the text above to the realm of architecture, our phoenix to be called back to life, again and again. So much about the eternal architecture? Does architecture ever exist in the present time? Is there a contemporary architecture? Or are the Future and the Past the only tenses for architecture that make sense?

My literary source – concerning Peter Brook and the traditions of theatre – gives some interesting etymology:

"An important point needs to be made at the very outset: the word 'tradition' (from the Latin 'tradere,' meaning 'to restore,' 'to transmit') carries within it a contradiction charged with repercussions. In its primary familiar usage, the word 'tradition' signifies 'a way of thinking or acting inherited from the past': it is therefore linked with the words 'custom' and 'habit.' In this sense, one might refer to an 'academic tradition,' to a 'Comédie Française tradition' or to 'Shakespearean tradition.'"

Coming all the way down to "custom", we are back in the definitions of "culture" – a system of standard situations, as defined by Christopher Alexander.

At this point, you must be mixed up already by my Shakespearean interpretations. Never mind, I want to touch another point which I have never really understood.

You write:

McLuhan's assertion that 'the medium is the message' and substitutes the personality cult of the (a) author. Can we not see a parallel context for architecture and the architect? In medieval architecture the medium is the message, but from the quattrocento onwards the identity of the architect becomes increasingly linked to the image of the work.

Yes, and here we come all the way to the present Fame-Game with its various play-rights and playwrights (See how lovely it is to play language-games with a language which is not one's own).

But: what has always confused me is that McLuhan speaks not of "message". I quoted this title recently and to be sure I took the book from my shelf and – damnit – he actually writes "the medium is the massage". Honestly, I cannot see his intention as clearly as if I had read "message" in this context. Some mental massage here, perhaps?

Playfully yours,
Mattikoo

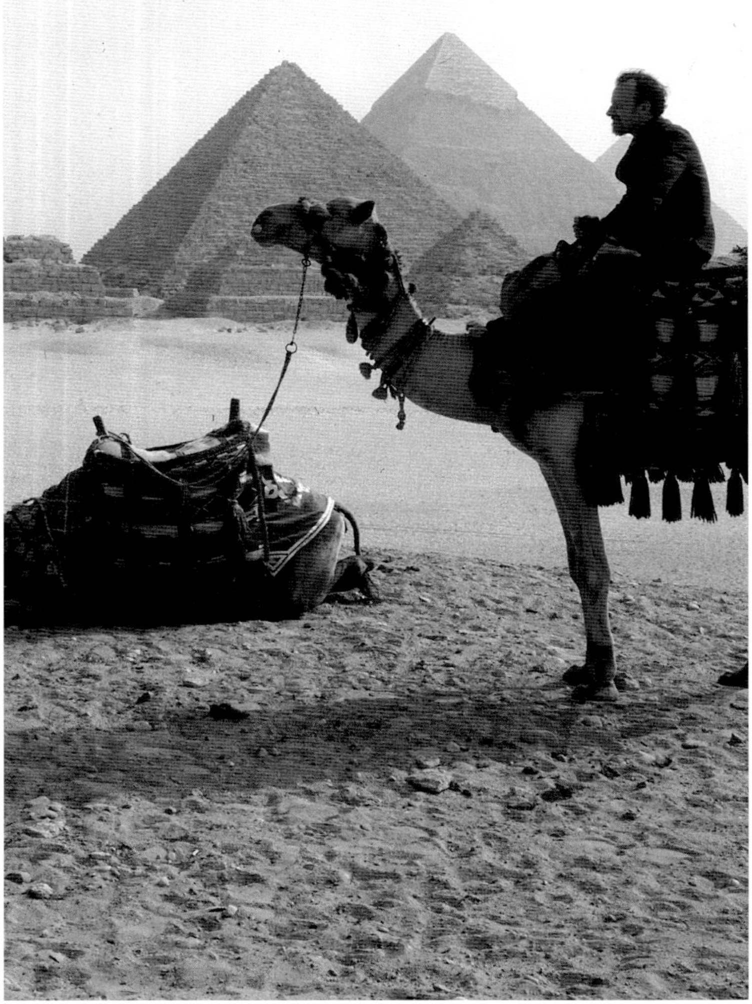

GEOMORPHIC WRINKLES

Matti K. Mäkinen

Is form an intelligible product of outer shape, apparent to the outer eye only? Or is there a deeper meaning infused into form from sources beyond man's apprehension?

Eliel Saarinen

Help me to surface, Malcolm.

Even in the dreams I am haunted by these Flutterbies, The Elephant I dare not mention…Sweating in my bed I have the ominous feeling that it is in here, somewhere in the dark. Remember the Indian story of the elephant in a dark room? And people whose game was to feel around with their hands, touch the animal and try to grasp what it was. One got hold of the tip of the tail and made his conclusions, the other one found the trunk and, reaching further, even the tusks. And so the spot-wise research covered large areas, but the ideas of the object of study could not be brought together to get the animal specified. One result could be confirmed: it had thousands of wrinkles. But the relation between surface and substance remained unsolved.

One possible way for Architecture to surface up from the dreams of modernism is now opening through the growing interest in the skin of the architectural body. There has been so much talk about the facades becoming thinner and thinner and leaving a shallowing depth for architecture to play its role. This way of progress – or regress? – can also be read as a message. It tells how the playground of the architect has been squeezed between the pressures of inside net space economy and outside limits set by town planning regulations.

Now we could ask how come the architect's realm does not reach to the inside of the building. It depends. A very visible example can be the office blocks. The rules for inside solutions are set by technical facilities, elevators and other arrangements for technical service, by administrative arrangements, by the standards of interior decoration – if you can call it decoration – et cetera. The time of office interiors like the fabulous Johnson Wax is long past.

And also past is the time of three-dimensional ornaments and statues in the exterior. They were turned to history already by the orthodoxy of early modernism. This sterilization was sealed through the development of building technology adjusted to the new bare bone architecture and secured by the seven locks of real estate economy. Technically, it would not need to be so expensive to mass-produce prefabricated saints and lions to elevate the facades, but under given circumstances the space needed would be far too expensive. Whether markets for this kind of industry were found is difficult to see, because it has not been tested. Some reference can be found, though, in the abundance of plastic Santa Clauses.

Although the early religious motifs as well as the sculptured plants and animals of the Art Nouveau are long since outdated, some inner urge for ornamentation seems to ask for satisfaction. The first modernists already based their designs on the artistic education they had received as part of the path towards their graduation as architects. If the rules of the 'ism' did not provide for beauty by decoration, then you sought your ways through concentrating your form-giving inventiveness on the structural or functional qualities of the building.

Now the masks have been thrown aside. It is time to dare, to break through. One of the ways of keeping on the sure side has been to start decorating the panes of the contemporary glassboxes. Even the function is easily found, that of safeguarding the Information, the holy secrets of Corporate and Administrative proceedings and documents. So, actually the silk printings developed to blur the newly found and officially manifested transparency of glass represent the purest functionalism you can think of. Still better, the most fashionable top artist can be hired to provide the patterns, if the client permits.

The body's biggest organ is the skin. The architects can feel relieved. Instead of losing both the interior and the third dimension of the exterior, we have found a gigantic 2-dimensional playground, a huge palette for artistic expression, legitimized by a revised concept of modernity and presented as a friendly gesture in the pattern books of the glass industry.

Surface is only a first step on a longer march. Seeking the support of a metaphor, you start analyzing the functions of the human skin. The idea of an anthropomorphic approach to architectural design opens a new level, offering our buildings an interactive interface. Your human skin is actually not intended for looking in and out through it. In this era of appearances, it is in an increasing degree rigged for looking at. The present fashion of skin tattooing, an art of story-telling, branding the identity of a modern breed of 'noble savages', occurs simultaneously with the silk printings or intensively coloured metal sheets on the buildings' facades. Is this a blind coincidence, or does it reflect something deeper, a hidden maelstrom in the flow of time?

The medium is the looks, be it pale, blushed or colored. But more primary are the skin's sensory functions, scanning temperatures, movements of air, caressing or painful touches, vibrations of hair-raising horror. Then there are the functions of fluid emissions, sweating, and the structural function of keeping the inside together, giving form and appearance to the sack of organs and protecting the contents, balancing the temperatures.

The interactive functions of the building's skin are still in the phase of preliminary studies. The visions include naturally ideas of blowing a new breath of life into the body of building, and designing the skin as an intermediator between this body and the outside environment. It is unnecessary to try guessing the opportunities this changing role of buildings provides for architectural expressions. An editorial of *Architectural Design* supports this view:

"The polarisation of ornament and structure that were first cast in stone by Vitruvius and perpetuated by the modernists no longer holds up. Computer modelling of integrated surfaces has usurped this bifurcation by blurring the inside and the outside, requiring new ways of considering tectonic form."[1]

But this is only one gate opened to welcome the renaissance of New Architecture. The first daredevils have already left the safe harbour of the modernist canon far behind and set a-sail exploring the possibilities to use skin as the supporting structure. Does the circle close here, have we moved from load-bearing exterior walls to post and lintel variations enclosed by a curtain wall, and has now the time come to give this skin a second thought and integrate – or re-integrate – it with the supporting structure? Yes and no. The circle closes but the ends do not meet. In the course of the process, the context has been changed and we have entered the digital era.

Along with the digital era comes digital architecture.

The first phase, the computerised design, has in a short time become capable of offering a comparative freedom of producing images of the most varying kinds. No wonder that so many architects have fallen for the temptation of a thoughtless play with shapes, colours and patterns, some random play without any deeper intentions, just to see whan the machine can do.

The second phase leads to a point where you stop the emergent movement on the screen with a wow-experience. This looks interesting...could it be a vision of some architecture? One line of these

[1] Helen Castle: Editorial, *Architectural Design*, 2/2003

studies leads to compositions of entangled stripes, and the next step, the idea of reading these forms as a kind of landscape is not so far-fetched.

The third phase is turning the dream into a design. What you need is a program, a competition or some other way to find a suitable problem to match the solution you have designed....not a building in the strictest sense but some formation between a landscape and a building. Is that architecture or geography? You don't know. But it melts fine into the given landscape and makes an integrated part of it. In a way, it is like an incarnation of ecology. And, through further development, it could be adopted to many functions of the built environments, even housing, or should I say habitation. We know that the prize-winners resulting from this kind of landscape-architecture philosophy have already seen daylight. Something has already been built, the Yokohama port terminal might serve as a contemporary example. If we start stepping back on the path of geomorphic architecture, we can remember the arcology and other studies of Paolo Soleri in the 1960s, or refer to Reima Pietilä, who at the same time in Finland took his long good-bye to functionalist forms, going further and further in his experiments of turning his buildings into integrated parts of nature. Or we can remember the old Mediterranian towns and villages, creeping up and down the steep hillsides, not to speak of the archaic phases of mankind, the people rigging up their homes in caves. Earth to earth, this is the way of man, as well as the past and future of his architecture.

The present phase of the geomorphic way of wrinkling the skin of our elephant architecture – if the trend takes on – is the most demanding. It would mean the heavy effort of turning the construction industry on to new tracks, where at least some part of the machinery would be developed for this new technology of building large skins, lined and folded to fit to the forms given by the topography of place. I bet that this would be a new step in computerizing the production processes.

Architecture, in its early phases, leaned towards imitations of nature. In the above, we have come close to this nature-architecture relation, finally inspired by the vistas opened by the computerized study of forms. In conclusion, we return to the words of Eliel Saarinen:

"Now then, what is form? Which are its primary characteristics? Is form an intelligible product of outer shape, apparent to the outer eye only? Or is there a deeper meaning infused into form from sources beyond man's [sic] apprehension? Or, to put it thus: is art soulless; or does it have a soul? The answer is obvious."[2]

[2] Eliel Saarinen, *The Search for Form in Art and Architecture*, Dover Publications, New York, 1985 (1948)

5 FINLANDIA

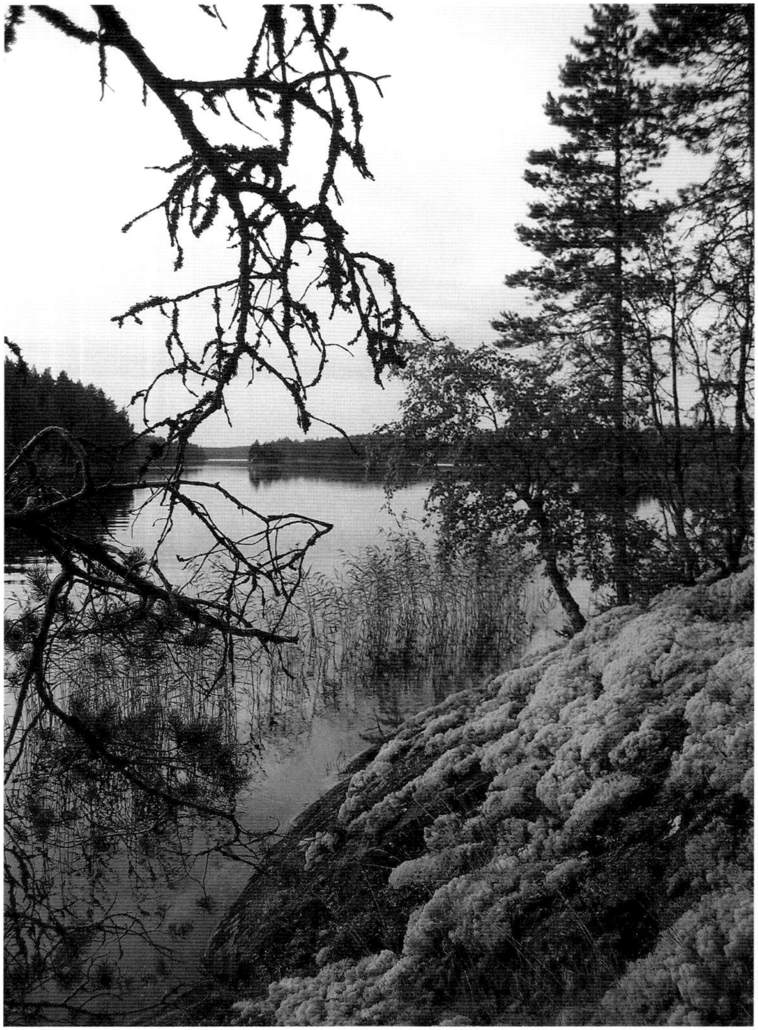

FINLANDIA: INTRODUZZIONE CON BRIO

Malcolm Quantrill

I set out from England's north-eastern Newcastle-upon-Tyne with Tony Walmsly, a fellow-student from Liverpool. Our voyage was in search of his 'Promised Land', the Finlandia he had discovered in 1952, the year of Helsinki's Olympic Games. Although it was June the initial rite of passage was memorable for the penetration of its cold and damp. How I pitied those poor Vikings clad only in their tinpot hats and rusty metal underwear. Fortunately, our journey was overnight, so we huddled together with our cheap whiskey and Guinness for warmth. Be of good cheer, we told each other: "Tomorrow will be Norway!"

We had but a few brief hours to steam the fatigue out from our unwashed flesh before land came in sight. At Bergen we were too tired to register much identity of the town. We boarded another boat, where we found that deck class included a free hose-down in our sleeping bags. Sodden, soggy, Viking blues. The only music was the pitter-patter of wetness. My last cigarette had drowned in an outer pocket. Those Viking oarsmen must have worn their spare parts thin as they strove to reach for warmer shores.

We slept in short, damp bursts, dreaming between the cut and thrust of fjords. Beauty blended with exhaustion in our hopes of better, drier times. And the bright morning brought the splash and shapely sparkle of Trondheim. So much wood splayed and formed into a virtual continuity of wall and roof. So many angles conspiring to conform to one pattern. From nature comes a quite natural architecture, seemingly by accident; a geometry born of familiarity and necessity – offering a humane mould that is both comfortable and persuasive.

Like all architecture, Trondheim is woven from materials of transition: the trees of the surrounding forest have been felled, cut and shaped to construct a gentle urbanity. The textures of its natural fabrics are echoed in every turn and pocket of the township. Yes! "Town's ship" is exactly right for Trondheim. A wooden vessel moored between sea and forest, a craft that floats at the very edges of existence, bridging from land-life to that of water. Even the fried herring that wait in the restaurant's trays to be purchased and eaten are conscripted to obey the order of the forest and its urban offspring. Town Ship!

Hitchhiking across Norway was rapid and almost without lasting impressions. It took only a couple of rides to reach the Gulf of Bothnia: the longer stretch of our journey to Sundsvaal was in an ever-graceful Citroen 'Light 15'. The driver of that low-slung French saloon was a young Norwegian engineer. His conversation came in short, rhythmic bursts, mimicking his deft handling of the Citroen's gear-stick. The car hugged the road affectionately, embracing some re-entrant corners before heading into the next stretch with a breathless kiss.

At one moment we were suspended above a ravine, the next we were climbing to a new and narrower height. Clearly the driver was familiar with every twist and turn. He welded each landscape prominence to the virtually invisible road with his skill. Fast mountain driving was a new experience for both of us: we were locked into a test of nerves, an initiation from which there was no escape. We had been taken on board for the ride, and this was the ride we were taken on. The Swedish end of that journey was smoother, more rolling, less exciting. Fields were like carpets, partially unrolled in an expansive welcome. We passed between broad corn fields, as the horizon dipped in more friendly proximity. There was certainly less variety in the landscape of Sweden than that of Norway, but it was not altogether a case of *Absolut* flatness!

Another ferry carried us across the Gulf of Bothnia, from Sundsvaal on the Swedish side to the Finnish port of Vaasa. It was necessary to ascend from the port to the level of Vaasa city proper. Ramps made this quite easy, although the first quarter hour of climbing did not seem to bring the city any closer. Just as we were becoming quite desperate for a glimpse of urban promise, a mere change of scale, or an increase in complexity, a lady appeared on the horizon.

With one hand she was waving a small flag, which we recognized as a Union Jack. At the same time she appeared to beckon us with her other arm. A friendly windmill of a person, both genuine and comic rolled into one. It was clear that she was moving, towards us, getting closer with each stride. In terms of advancing the cause of proximity she was obviously making more progress than the city itself. Already within earshot, she began to call out to us in strong, deep tones.

She was wearing a white blouse, crisply starched and her generous bosom was exercising vigorously beneath its bold, firm panels. What I heard was less of a shout and more of a mezzo-soprano aria. There was further evidence of her rhythmic bosom accompanied by the flapping of white shirt applause. Finally, I distinctly heard her say: "I am Madame Ramsay. Teacher of English. Not English teacher. But Finnish teacher of English". She took a deep breath before adding. "Welcome to Finland. Welcome to our country".

By then she was upon us, breathing heavily in starchy waves, smothering us with warm and perfumed kisses. "Are you sailors?" she wanted to know, and answered herself without waiting: "No, you are not sailors". We told her we were students. "You understand," she pronounced, laughing: "I have taught English language to sailors". We laughed with her to show good will. And beckoning us to follow her she concluded: "My husband was sea captain. I am the wife of a roving man. Yes? You see, he sails the oceans wide. As for me, I am his anchor here at home".

The captain did not speak English, only Swedish. But he carried on a sort of conversation through a series of harmonious grunts. This was extremely helpful because it taught us to distinguish between Finnish and Swedish at an early stage of our visit. Also, one of Walmsley's promises was fulfilled in Vaasa. He had boasted of the superlative quality of blonde and blue-eyed Finnish girls. Of course Mrs Ramsay didn't qualify. She was already a matron and a late-blooming brunette at that. But the promise of the unique Finnish strawberry came true, as we gorged helping after helping of the sweet little berries, helped down by the great scopes of vanilla ice-cream Madame Ramsay dished out.

As we enjoyed ourselves Captain Ramsay brought his vocabulary of sympathetic grunts to a fever pitch. "He is retelling his favourite story," Madame Ramsay explained. "It concerns the true secret of Finnish ice-cream, which is that it's made not just from the best milk of our fine Finnish cows, but depends upon the addition of a most important ingredient – some milk squeezed from the breasts of the milkmaids themselves". She turned away to hide her sudden blush. Her cheeks assumed the color of the strawberries. While the whiteness of her shirt intensified, as though to underline her innocence. "That is the meaning of our Finnish *Liebfraumilch*", she confided.

We hardly expected that our path south from Vaasa to Jyväskylä would pass through neatly cultivated fields of those blue-eyed beauties that were vaunted as the region's natural crop. Perhaps we resembled a caricature of the conqueror Cortez as we set out with our little Union Jack fluttering from Walmsley's rucksack. It had, of course, been Madame Ramsay's flag. She had forced it upon us as we left her home, saying: "Perhaps it will bring you good fortune on your journey. In any case, my people admire the British and this little flag will remind them to be on their best behavior when they meet you".

Madame Ramsay was a prophetess indeed, for within little more than fifty kilometres from Vaasa, as we were looking out for a ride, a large American car passed us, stopped suddenly, then went into reverse to retrace its path. It drew alongside us to reveal a man in late-middle age. He was not exactly fat, rather squat with generously padded limbs. His companion was a woman, perhaps a little younger, who quickly jumped out of the car and embraced Walmsley.

Whenever threatened by a woman intent on kissing him, Walmsley broke out into a cold sweat and began to shake from head to toe. Nobody has been able to explain the cause of his behaviour, although it has been suggested that it is connected with the fact that he was brought up as a Methodist. Ignoring his shakes, the woman slapped Walmsley on the back, or more precisely the flag on his backpack. The liquid phrases she exchanged with her companion confirmed that they spoke Finnish rather than Swedish.

We were hurriedly bundled into the car which then sped off down the road. The woman continued to hold onto our Union Jack, patting it affectionately. And soon we arrived at a farm. There we were waited on by dumpy, female servants, peasant women of uncertain age who brought coffee and milk and bread and cheese. In no time at all we were joined by a tall, good-looking man in his late- thirties. "I am Captain Puutanen," he said, "and I help fly Mr Karhumäki's aeroplanes". He explained that our host was one of Finland's pioneer aeronauts, and it so happened that the couple had a daughter who was in England, where she was about to study English. Hence the significance of our Union Jack and the reason we had been whisked off to their home. Captain Puutanen had been summoned to look after us, to ensure translation of Karhumäki's much repeated questions, and to keep us company for the rest of the day.

It was Saturday and the afternoon proceeded to extend itself into the evening without interruption. The interminable Finnish mid-Summer day was upon us, its continuity holding all thoughts of night and darkness at bay. After we had eaten an endless repetition of morning snacks, Captain Puutanen summoned us to join him for a walk through the woodlands along one border of the property. "You are very fortunate", he told us, "because today is Saturday. That means we will take *sauna* this evening. And I invite you to join me now and go down to the bathhouse so we can check that everything has been prepared for us".

We wandered with him along the woodland fringe, an area mostly populated by slender young birches. The sauna itself was like a small cottage. It had three rooms: the outer "dressing" chamber; an inner "wash" room and the sauna (or hot chamber) itself. Walking, wandering in and out of the trees seemed without purpose, yet it was relaxing and hinted at the some mysterious process.

Suddenly the Captain stopped and, dropping slowly to his knees, retrieved a piece of birch-bark from the ground. It was about a foot long and curled inwards around the missing branch it had recently wrapped. "*Sauna* is the Finnish bath", the Captain informed us. "But it is more than just a bath", he continued, "because it is a ritual that links Man and Nature".

The pilot went on to emphasize that since it is a ritual, there is nothing automatic about preparation for the *sauna.* He continued his role as our guide, by telling us that by the enactment of *sauna,* one's participation in its ritual requires an understanding of its symbolic form and meaning. It is necessary to realize how nature frames and forms our ritual enactments. There is a direct link between *sauna* and the most original sources of society, its rituals and formal expressions. Of course, the element of fire occurs naturally in the forest, when the hot sun kindles the dry tinder of dead trees. There can be no sauna without fire. In a symbolic sense, we are out here in the Karhumäki woods, looking for fire, seeking out its source. And we have found it in this piece of dried birch-bark. "This means", he suggested, "that we are now only a Boy Scout away from combustion".

But it appears that, within the Karhumäki *sauna* rubric, Boy Scouts play no active part. Instead, we had to gather armfuls of birch-bark, followed by even greater quantities of small, broken branches and twigs of birch. And it took half and hour to prepare the careful arrangement and the stacking of wood and bark beneath the oven of stones in the inner chamber of the *sauna.* A further hour passed while the stones were fiercely scorched by the fire's dying embers.

Perhaps only thirty to forty-five minutes were actually spent enjoying the heat. This was frequently made more intense when the pilot judiciously ladled water onto the stones, and waves of overpowering super-heated steam thrashed against our eager bodies. It was quite curious the way our bodies became liquid, that is, the entire area of skin seemed to melt and gleam with a glaze of wetness.

It is the "meaning" of the *sauna* to remove us from the fatiguing realities of this world and transport our minds and bodies to a different, higher plane. After bearing the *sauna*'s unbearable heat my body was fatigued in quite a different way. It felt as though each pore had been individually cleansed, as if by some divine intervention. While the inner man craved bottle after bottle of sparkling mineral water, I felt the body itself sparkling.

And then I could no longer help it. I totally failed to resist the onslaught of sleep. It was only on waking two hours later was I let into the biggest secret of all. I had actually been sleeping in the bed used by Marshal Mannerheim when he had come to stay in the house. And so my perfect first *sauna* came to an end. After a *sauna* fit for a king, I had slept in the bed of a hero.

Today, fifty years later, I no longer have a chance to pursue the ritual perfection of my initial *sauna* at the Karhumäki's house, but the memory of that original initiation lingers on and strengthens my resolve to continue my practice of taking a *sauna,* however little that may resemble the wonderful original, at least three times a week.

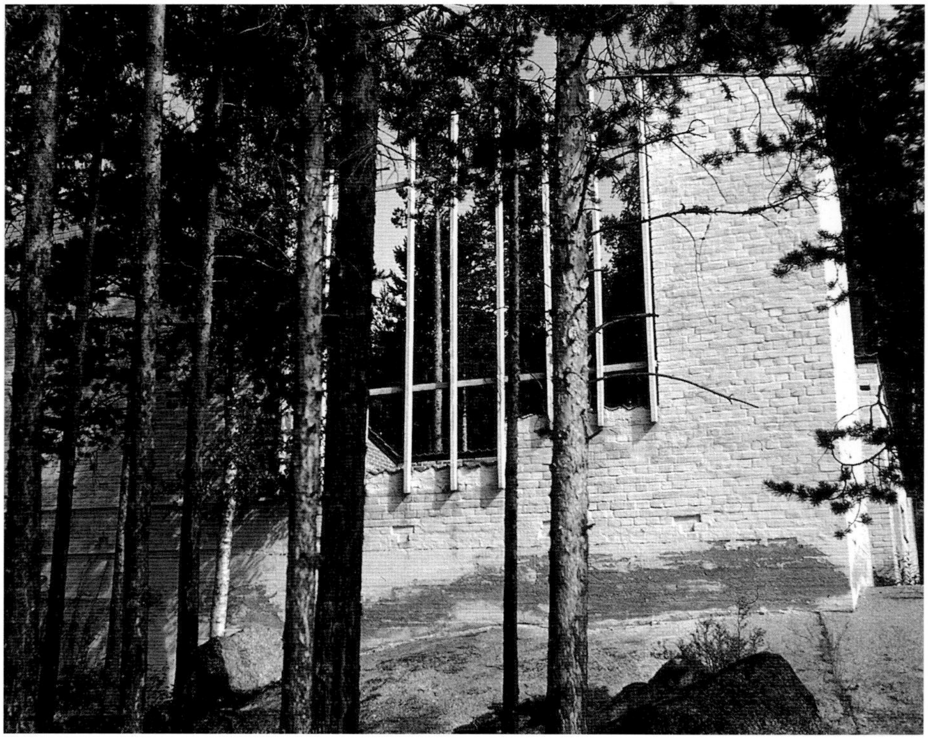

MALCOLM IN WONDERLAND – INTERVIEW FACE TO FACE

Matti K. Mäkinen – Malcolm Quantrill

It's the 17th November 2003, in Espoo, Finland, and we are trying to tape an interview with Malcolm Quantrill.

MKM: Okay, Malcolm, here we sit. It's a rainy November day outside and my first question is about your childhood. Where did you live as a child? And in what kind of family, and how did you come to understand that you wanted to study architecture?

MQ: Well, first of all I was born in Norwich on the east coast of England, just immediately north east of London. My father was a shoemaker and my mother worked occasionally, but she was mostly in the home. I am an only child and I was fortunate to gain access to the local Grammar School, which was the gateway to university entrance at that time. But at about the age of thirteen or so, I became very interested in architecture.

MKM: And now we are sitting here in Finland; after many long years we return to your young days. One of those days you decided to come to Finland. How did it happen and where had you been before that, outside of England?

MQ: Well, the first place I went to out of England was at the end of my Grammar School days, which would have been in 1947. I went to Lille in France and took part in a Semaine de Culture Francaise to polish up my French with the idea of passing the entrance examination for the university.

MKM: Excuse me. Had you studied French at school?

MQ: Yes. It was the only other language I studied. I did a little bit of Latin at the very end of my school days, so it was really too late to be useful. But French I always managed reasonably well. For a number of reasons when I left the school I didn't go straight to university. I was apprenticed; I became an articled pupil to an architect in Norwich and I worked with him for three years. During that period I made two visits to Holland. I was very interested in Dutch architecture, in particular the work of Dudok. During that period, I have to confess I also had a Dutch girlfriend but she didn't live in an area which was rich in modern architecture. So that relationship didn't last. The idea of architecture lasted longer than the girlfriend.

MKM: And at some point you decided to go to Finland. When was that, what time of the year was it, which way did you come and did you have some company with you when you arrived?

MQ: Yes. First of all, I was one of the promising students of Colin Rowe. He left Liverpool University to become a Professor at Cornell, where he spent most of his later years. Rowe expected his bright students to go and spend a long summer (8 to 12 weeks) in Italy. So in the summer of 1953 I was all prepared to go to Italy, when suddenly the top student in our class Tony Walmsley said to me "Look, why would you want to go to Italy which is always packed with people?" He suggested instead: "Why don't you come with me to Finland? I was there last year. It was the year of Olympic Games, 1952. Finnish girls are very beautiful and in the summer they also have these fantastic strawberries and ice cream."

MKM: That summer of 1953 I was working as an apprentice in an architecture office in Helsinki and we had a couple of English students working there at that time. It was part of the beginning of my knowledge of English, which I learned by talking with them at the drafting table.

MQ: Could you have realized that it was us? It was Tony and me! What happened was this. We came to Finland from Newcastle. First we went by ship to Bergen and then took a boat up to Trondheim. We hitchhiked across Norway and Sweden and took the ferry across from Sundsvall to Vaasa, where we were met by a very charming lady who spoke English. Her husband had been a sea captain. We continued hitching down to Jyväskylä and then went on to Säynätsalo to see Aalto's new town hall.

MKM: Then you were really in Finland… What were your intentions? Did you want to take a break or did you go sort of architectural sightseeing? What was your great idea? How did you manage for money?

MQ: Ha! Well, you see, we had to earn our living somehow that summer. We didn't have enough money for the whole summer. So, if we didn't get job we would have had to turn tail and gone back to England. It was the most extraordinary expedition because after we left Vaasa and continued hitchhiking, a car stopped suddenly and the couple explained in very broken English that they had a daughter studying in England and they would like to help us. This man happened to be Niilo Karhumäki who owned the KarAir airline and he invited us back to their home. We stayed with them and my first sauna was at Niilo Karhumäki's home with one of the KarAir pilots who spoke English and had been summoned by his boss to help us. After we spent the weekend with them we continued on to Jyväskylä, and then on to Säynätsalo. We were busily absorbing Aalto's town hall, when this very charming business man appeared from nowhere and asked whether we were interested in the work of Alvar Aalto? We told him: "Yes, very much". And he said "Do you know he has built a house near here? It is a very funny house because it doesn't have any windows. But if you want to see it I'll help you get there". He took us to a point in the forest and said, pointing with his hand, if you go straight for about four kilometres you will come to Alvar Aalto's new house.

MKM: Did your find your way?

MQ: Yes, we did. All the way the meadows were full of cows. So our feet got very clogged with cow shit, you know? But eventually we came to the back door of the Muuratsalo house. We arrived in the summer of 1953, and the house was finished a few weeks before that.

Now, my friend Tony was a Methodist so he had some religious principles, some moral attitudes. I told him; here we are in this garden, belonging to Aalto and his family. And we should knock on the door and tell them we are here. And he replied "Oh wait a minute we should take some pictures first and then we can knock. Just in case they won't let us take pictures". Well, there we were in the garden of that Muuratsalo house and I repeated to Tony: "We are on private property. We should tell Professor Aalto that we are here. Then, at that moment to our great surprise, Elissa Aalto came out of the back door wearing nothing but a towel around her head. She shook the table cloth and danced back inside. I had the telephoto lens on my camera but I didn't take the picture. Elissa and I often joked about this later. Anyway, we then went to the door knocked. Professor Aalto came to the door and, after we had introduced ourselves, invited us in. His first question was "Where did you leave your boat?" When we explained that we didn't have a boat he said: "That is impossible. I built this house so you can only come here from Säynätsalo by boat across the lake". So we told him: "We actually walked here from Säynätsalo". "Oh the damned English, there is no stopping them", he replied and he insisted we stay for lunch. But since they had no food in the house we had to take Aalto's boat and go across to Säynätsalo to buy salami and cheese, and bread, and wine so we could have lunch. I still have the photograph of the house interior, looking towards this suspended studio. And there are the packages of food which we had just collected from Säynätsalo.

MKM: Well, so this was Säynätsalo but, how long was your stay in Finland altogether at the time?

MQ: Well, we came in June and we stayed two months, the whole of June and July and just into August. When we got to Helsinki we looked for a job but we didn't find one easily. We happened to go into a shop which had just recently opened. It was called Marimekko, and there I met this extraordinary woman: she was really extraordinary. She had one earring and it was very large, I would say about 8cm in diameter hanging down from one ear. Her name seemed quite poetic, too. She said: "Oh well, if you can't get into one of the private offices you should try Rakennushallitus to get a good job". And so we went there, to the Finnish National Board of Public Building, and … Well you see, we went there and we were standing in this office, which seemed to be entirely populated by women architects. And they were apparently saying in Finnish, "These two English men look quite good. We should take them; we need some men in this office". So we got a job there in Rakennushallitus, I think we worked there for about 10 weeks.

MKM: You know there was a reason why all those ladies worked there. Many of them were very competent architects. But, for a woman at that time it was not so easy to start a private practice without a man, so they ended up at these offices of public service and the men kept active the private offices.

MQ: We settled into that office, staying in Domus Acatemica as our lodging. And what I shouldn't forget is the fact that Niilo Karhumäki had told us that when we had settled in Helsinki we should contact his office and arrange for a complementary flight to the north of Finland. And so we did, and we flew up to Rovaniemi. It was a weekend, and we had a wonderful time there. We went up with all these fishermen and they all had fishing rods and so forth, and when we got there we were told "unfortunately the planes are full, and so you have to go back by train" and that was a very memorable experience because it was the smokiest train I've ever taken. On the way back we were fumigated by this engine which burned wood. It took us, I don't remember how long, maybe 36 hours or something like that. We arrived late in Helsinki. So, we had to explain ourselves on Tuesday morning to the lady architects of Rakennushallitus. But they were all very kind and generous about it.

MKM: So what kind of an idea did you get at that time of the landscape, the people and so on? How was Finland in the early 1950s?

MQ: Well, I spoke about going earlier to France and there I stayed with a family. In Holland, too, I had an experience of family life too. In Finland we didn't have that exactly, although almost everybody invited us to their homes. The ladies in the office invited us to go and have strawberries or whatever, to have a picnic or something like that.

MKM: Does that mean that you have a feeling that the Finns are friendly?

MQ: Yes, Finns very much wanted to be friendly. They gave the impression that they had been rather isolated, which they didn't want to be. They had been cut off by the Second World War and many circumstances in history and they really wanted to be welcoming. For the most part the difficulty was that English was not even their third language after Finnish and Swedish. German was their third language and English only their fourth. And this was a bit of a problem since I didn't speak any German at that time.

MKM: Yes, I agree. That was the sort of dominating generation at the time.

MQ: But during the time I was there we saw Aalto again in his Helsinki office and Armi Ratia was especially generous. I went many times to her apartment. She lived in that place overlooking the harbour close to St. Henrik's Church, where she had an apartment. Also at that time, in that same area where the ferry terminal for Sweden is now, Aarne Ervi had his office. That was before his divorce, when he was still quite wealthy. So I visited him and I saw him twice in that office, and I had the feeling that this was the place that I'd come to see, then go away and never see him again. I had the impression that I'd be back, I would have to return because there was something quite magnetic about Finland, although the language was always a problem and continues to be so. But I can understand what Tony Walmsley wanted to say when he said how impressed he'd been when he came for the Olympic Games and shared with me the enthusiasm that he had known before.

MKM: Yes, you happened to bump into Finland at a time when, as we have seen afterwards, Finnish architecture had its, how to say, heyday, and it just happened to come in at that time. I think I understand that you could not see that it happened in that short period because you could not see the future…

MQ: I must say that, well, this was '53 and I didn't come back to Finland until '57, at that time I had been in the United States for, well I went to the United States in 1954 after I graduated and I got a Fulbright Fellowship at the University of Pennsylvania to study with Louis Kahn and McCarg and Paul Rudolf, and so when I came back to Finland in '57 it was somehow different. Partly I had become very friendly with that delightful woman, she was a widow in the United States, she was also a Fulbright scholar, she was an economist, and we had a very close relationship because I came back and spent quite a bit of the summer with her in '57, and I saw Kyllikki again and we had the wonderful times that she always created, you know, they were wonderful get-togethers.

MKM: Excuse me, there is something I didn't get: the woman you got acquainted with, and who was your friend. Was she Finnish?

MQ: Yes, she was a Finnish Fulbright scholar and I met her in Philadelphia. It was a complete accident because I didn't bump into any other Finns, but I bumped into this woman. And because I knew a bit about Finland, and she was surprised to find somebody who knew about her homeland we became good friends.

MKM: Yes, it is only natural that you met her in Philadelphia, because Philadelphia in my estimation is about the most Finnish place in America.

MQ: Well, that could be. Anyway, we had a good time together and I remember that this lady had to have very good quality shoes. So I was persuaded to bring back these shoes from England. My mother was very surprised, she said: "How can you choose shoes for a woman you don't know?" I said "Well, I know her rather well", and I did. So, I bought the shoes to Kyllikki, who said: "When you go back to America, you should go on one of the Finnish freighters, and how they had this way of arranging things so that nobody would know that they were together. There were several ways, you see, of moving from one part of the ship to another. Anyway, I went back on this freighter and I was the only male passenger, the other eleven were women, and I fell in love with the youngest of them. We had our first date in Lübeck. She spoke some German. She eventually became my wife. We had this date in Lübeck, then we corresponded for a year. Then she came to Louisiana where I was teaching at Louisiana State University. We married there in 1958 and then came back to Finland in 1959. I'd been given a place at that time in the office of Aarne Ervi.

MKM: How long did that marriage last?

MQ: Oh, it lasted from '58 to '65…

MKM: Well, that is a typical age for a marriage, so they say…

MQ: Well, in 1959 when I was here again, I don't know how aware I was of the changes, the transitions in Finnish architecture. Of course a lot of the work that interested me, like the Vuoksenniska Church and the House of Culture and so forth, had been completed. And there was a very good body of Aalto brick buildings coming out of his experience of Baker House at MIT. But Armi Ratia, who was always provocative, said to me "Malcolm, why are you always so interested in Alvar Aalto? I mean, he really belongs to the '30s you know, and you should be more interested in what's going on right now, in the present generation of Finnish architects, in Reima Pietilä, for example. I will introduce you to him if you would like that". And I said yes of course I would very much like it. So after a couple of days she called me and she said, "You have to go on Friday afternoon at four o'clock to the English Tea Room, and there you will find Reima Pietilä. Normally I would send people to the Rautatalo Cafe, but to meet Reima Pietilä you can't go to the Rautatalo because that is Aalto territory, so you have to go to the English Tea Room instead".

MKM: That was quite an early time to get acquainted with Reima…

MQ: Oh yes, because in 1958 he had completed the Finnish Pavillion for the Brussels World Fair, and he had recently won the Kaleva Church competition for Tampere. He arranged for me to contribute to *Le Carré Bleu* later and I wrote a couple of pieces for that publication. I was not really much in touch with Finnish architecture for most of the '60s. In 1974, however, I had registered to go to Madrid for the UIA conference. But I didn't go because I was sick. Reima saw my name in the list of participants, and he didn't find me in Madrid, so he wrote to me and as a result of that I got back in touch with him and my work in Finland started all over again from 1974. I was very much indebted to Reima for this second cycle.

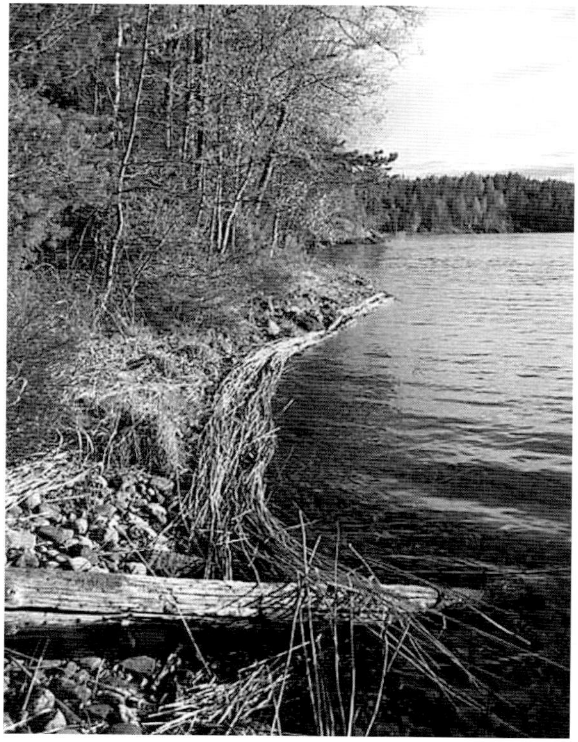

MKM: If you count all the time you have spent in Finland from the early beginning until now, how long have you been connected to my country?

MQ: Well, I was in Helsinki the best part of three months in '53. Then I was here about a month in '57, so that's four months. And then we arrived here in June '59 and left again in June '60, so that was another twelve months, so that was a year and four months. And I've been here various times since; so I guess it's been something in excess of two years all together.

MKM: So your I might call it *Finnishness*, derived of course from your family relations and things like that, but then on the other hand, you are very renowned, especially by Finnish architects, for your books, which are very much respected here. But where else do you have some sort of roots or a strong attraction?

MQ: Well, that's a really difficult question. I mean, I've written a little bit about English architecture but not very much. Finnish architecture has been an important part of my overall education and my development as a mature architect and thinker. I believe that I can never repay this debt. I am writing quite a lot about Latin American architecture these days. But I'm also writing about the architecture of Nova Scotia, which comes close to the idea of Finland. I often joke that when I go to Finland, the land is rather flat and there is a pine forest and you put your hand out and it's in the Baltic; while when I'm in Nova Scotia the landscape also is rather flat and there is also a pine forest, but when you put your hand out it's in the Atlantic. So I do see a connection between my experience in Finland and now my explorations in Canada.

But there is no connection to Latin America. Latin America is a new discovery for me, but my education in architecture has little to do really with its roots in England, except that I think I became an architect because of the influence of Christopher Wren. But, my interest has always been abroad and after Dudok, it was then Finnish architecture and, as I said to you earlier today, if a book about Kristian Gullichsen had not been written then I would have to write that, because I consider him to be one of the really worthy architects in the Finnish tradition and I would like to support his position in this evolution.

MKM: Sure, but very often, especially of course in this country, but also elsewhere, you can hear of this great Finnish architecture, and you have spoken of that, given lectures on that and written about it over the decades. So how would you describe Finnish architecture as a concept, with a few words, can it be described? I believe this is a nasty question.

MQ: Well, it is a difficult question but not an impossible one, because the idea of *genius loci*, that my late friend Norberg-Schulz was so vigorous in pursuing, is probably best demonstrated in Finland and by Finnish work. Of course, you have spoken about the international influences, and that's quite right, take somebody like Viljo Revell, by the time he did the Toronto Town Hall. Can you describe this anymore as a Finnish work? Would you know that this could be an expression of Finnish thought? Would you know for certain that this idea came from a Finnish architect? I am not at all sure about that.

MKM: Maybe at that time, when it was designed, if you looked at the Miesian highrises nearby in Toronto, you could see the difference.

MQ: Perhaps it still has an individuality which was not characteristic of the modern movement; so I think that the idea of clear thinking about a modern way of life and the use of good materials, and the escape from historicism; well, it is this idea of simplicity of form a very direct approach, very pure use of materials, and yet this does not add up to a kind of international style. If you ask me is Rovaniemi airport typical of Finnish modern architecture, I would have to say not really. It is rather part of the bridge that Finnish architecture is building between itself and the new internationalism?

MKM: Yes, but here we come to the function of an airport, which may be the intentional building of a bridge between international reality and this one here in Finland.

MQ: It may not be a very good example from that point of view because in an airport you are not any longer establishing a *genius loci*, a sense of place.

MKM: Yes, and you can have all these explanations that I have given you…

MQ: It is not a question of establishing the status quo, either.

MKM: It is the same with embassies by the way, the complicated question of national identity. Should it be of the land where the embassy is going to be or should it be the identity of Finland? I have met many cases of this because I've been sitting in those embassy competition juries.

MQ: Reima Pietilä said, I think about New Delhi, this is a Finnish island in the Indian archipelago. He was aware of this problem, and it is a very difficult one indeed.

MKM: I had very interesting discussions in Berlin, with the local German architects when we had to make the Scandinavian embassies and the Finnish embassy there. We came to the question of the Berlin identity. But then came also the question of the Finnish identity and so on, and the eventual clash between these two. My question is still about Finnish identity, and the Finnish people, and not only the first time you met them but, say, as an experience from all of these years you have met the Finns in their country and elsewhere. It's over to you.

MQ: Well, of course, we shouldn't make generalizations; my English teacher always said "all generalizations are false, including this one". Therefore, talking about what are the characteristics of Finns, I have to be very cautious, but I am going to say that there has been represented to me the idea of Finnish architecture made by different Finnish architects in their own ways, whether they were Aalto or Pietilä or Gullichsen, or more recently Helin and Siitonen or my good friend Juha Leiviskä. There is one side of the situation where the "clothing" of the architecture is characteristically Finnish. This is why I have come to understand it as Finnish architecture. And then I have to go back to my good friend Tony Walmsley, who told me that one of the advantages of going to Finland in 1953 was not only to see the architecture of Alvar Aalto and other Finnish architects, but also to meet those delightful women. And I indeed met them and they were not clothed in some pretence, whether that was about a national style or form. But I remember very well all three of the women I had very important relations with, and they came to me without clothing, without pretence, without any camouflage of their female form.

MKM: Yes, if you think of the traditional way of describing Finland as a nation, as a country, so it is a *she*, it is a woman, it is a young woman, especially in the connections of the early 1900s, when Finland still was linked to Russia: so there was the Russian bear trying to catch the young Finnish maiden. And on those occasions she had her dress on rather tightly, you might say.

MQ: Well, the currency that I remember from the '50s or the '60s showed this parade of naked people printed across the banknotes. And Finns used to laugh and say that this is the Finnish nation after she had been dealt with by the Russians. The Finns no longer had anything left to wear.

MKM: Yes, that banknote was designed by Eliel Saarinen so…

MQ: Nevertheless, it was still representative of the economic situation after the Second World War.

MKM: In this globalizing world, you easily come to question the meaning of a national architecture, such as Finnish architecture, Swedish architecture, English architecture, Japanese architecture, so it's not so difficult to come to the idea that maybe these national characters are in the act of work, and is it especially so when we talk about Finnish architecture. Do you think that it has a future as Finnish, as something that has a taste and flavour of this nation? And just what is this Finnish flavour in architecture?

MQ: I think there are a number of issues here. The first issue to me is one of craftsmanship, that is what is so poor, what is bad in so much of today's architecture with its dependence upon the computer.

MKM: Excuse me Malcolm, you said something about the use of the computer and its influence in architecture: would you please explain?

MQ: Yes, the difficulty really is in understanding the relationship between the real and the abstract. And the computer is an abstract means for realizing ambitions in architectural terms, but it is only a means, it is not the solution, it's not the complete diagram, and that is why I stress the idea of craftsmanship. This is very important for students who are going to become architects. Unless they understand this material presence of architecture they will never be able to make it, because the computer does not understand it, the computer is merely a tool between ourselves and the realization of our dreams.

MKM: May I interrupt you a moment, just to think about certain devices, like for instance the T-square, that have very strongly influenced architecture? Have they given or limited the possibilities of the kinds of architecture we can produce?

MQ: Well, I'd like to refer here to a recent lecture given by Professor Marco Frascari, who was talking about the horizon of the drafting board, how far can you reach out when you are drawing on the traditional drawing board and what is the difference when you are drawing as it were through the computer, and I think that there is a very important relationship, because you extend beyond the original horizons of the drafting table. But that doesn't mean that you now have complete control of what happens beyond those original horizons. That's what I want to stress, this knowledge about our determination to come to grips with the detail of the column, of the capital, of the junction between the column and the beam, what happens to the door frame, you know, all of these things without which architecture doesn't actually exist.

MKM: There seems to be a new kind of situation through the fact that we are sort of made to jump out of the two-dimensional reality of the drafting board, onto the three-dimensional reality – or is it unreality or the illusion of the cyberspace of the computer?

MQ: Well, I can only explain this, or exercise my concern about this, in the following way. Yes, you are right, we have moved from two-dimensionality to three-dimensionality, but this only means that instead of having two lines crossing we have three lines crossing and what happens where those 3 lines cross is a matter of great importance, because this is what the computer does not fill in. If you don't have knowledge about that intersection of the three lines then you can't make three-dimensional architecture. So okay, we move from the two-dimensional to the three-dimensional but the three-dimensional poses problems which have to be pondered by the architect, by human beings, which cannot be contemplated by the damned machine.

MKM: On the other hand, there is the danger that if the use of computer makes you sort of lazy because the computer makes it too easy to produce shapes and forms and imaginary pictures of these and that, which would cause more pain if you make it by pen alone or the use of traditional tools, but now they come very easily. The computer has an imagination of its own when it produces the pictures and then you just have to make your choice between them: what do you say of that?

MQ: Well, I would say what I've been saying for a long time, which is that brain surgery is not easy and architecture is no easier than brain surgery. It's something you really have to learn with a lot of intensive study, so you throw away the pencil and use the computer, that doesn't release you from the obligation of acquiring all the knowledge and experience that is necessary to make that junction between the column and the beam, if that's going to be a capital. Something has to be there, and the computer does not know what that something is. It simply does not know. You have to feed in the required information so that it will realize itself in that detail, because without that sense of detail architecture doesn't exist.

MKM: In other words we have to be careful that we do not fall for the temptations offered by the computer.

MQ: Well, of course the computer is an invaluable tool. I mean, it would be crazy on my part to suggest that we just get rid of the computer and pretend that we are carrying on as we did in the '20s and '30s. That is not the suggestion at all. What I want to say is that the computer is a tool, we have to learn how to use this tool, we have to realize that only through our own sophistication and our own applications can we make the tool help us realize our dreams.

MKM: Well then, let's take another angle and have a couple on words on the state of urban planning in Finland. It has been said that it doesn't achieve the higher level of Finnish architecture, as it has been assessed, so it may occur only in single buildings in free locations, or in the forest. But what about the relation to a larger entity, to the community, to the urban plan? What would you say about that?

MQ: It could be this revolutionary view of urban planning as a single building jumping up and sprouting out in the forest. But perhaps it could be that this "naturalistic" view is not really very well informed, I mean, of course, Säynätsalo Town Hall would be an example of that sort of thing. But it is equally true that buildings comprising the architecture of Finland, as we have known it, from the end of the 19th century to the present, just as much depends upon an urban context into which it grows canonically. The problem is that – and this is not just a problem for Finland, it's a universal problem – whereas in the Renaissance you could have an ideal city, and so you planned the overall form, even in the remodelling of Vienna when the whole Ringstrasse was developed, now the idea of creating a form is so difficult, and I invented this term for Aalto's, contribution because I think it was important that he designed his rather ragged and carefree buildings, and I came to think of them as his "urban fragments". But you see, even this is not entirely helpful because you have to organize the fragments into a coherent whole. Efforts to do this, like the plan by James Stirling to create an urban context by using the plan forms of the fortresses and cathedrals and other building types are not helpful either.

We are not able at the moment to understand the individual piece in relationship to the whole, and I think that Finland has suffered only as badly from this problem as the rest of the Western world.

MKM: Well it seems to me that then we – once again – return to this definition by Siegfried Giedion, architecture being an interpretation of the way of life valid for our period, and if we lift this up to the level of town planning, urban planning, you mentioned the word 'fragment'. So it may as well be that this fragmentation of life is measured in the shape that town planning is taking. What do you say about that?

MQ: The problem, if you view the growth of the city from the Middle Ages to the present, is that there is always this kind of AC-DC business, alternating current, or direct current. The idea that the city has no form, but the form becomes itself is a medieval idea. You know it has certain centres, but the form is the form that it takes. Then you put a wall around it. But that wall is an inadequate enclosure of the campus, as it were, so you extend it by having *fauxbourgs*, extensions of the city outside the wall. Then you have the Renaissance idea, which starts out with an ideal form. But that doesn't go very far because the ideal form is only good as a concept: it isn't really good as an operation. So life proceeds and with the industrial revolution and rolling through the 18th century and the 19th century we get up to date, and there still isn't any system, which is supported by legislation, which is supported by society, which allows us to make a city that conforms to the ambitions and to the aggressiveness of our modern society. That's the difficulty. We can have very good ideas but we get lousy results, because we are not able to coordinate those ideas within permissible limits.

MKM: Well Malcolm, I think the time has come to thank you for the picture you have given through your wide-angle lens of Finnish architecture and Finnish urban planning. We have deserved our dinner now, thank you very much.

MQ: Thank you, Mattikoo!

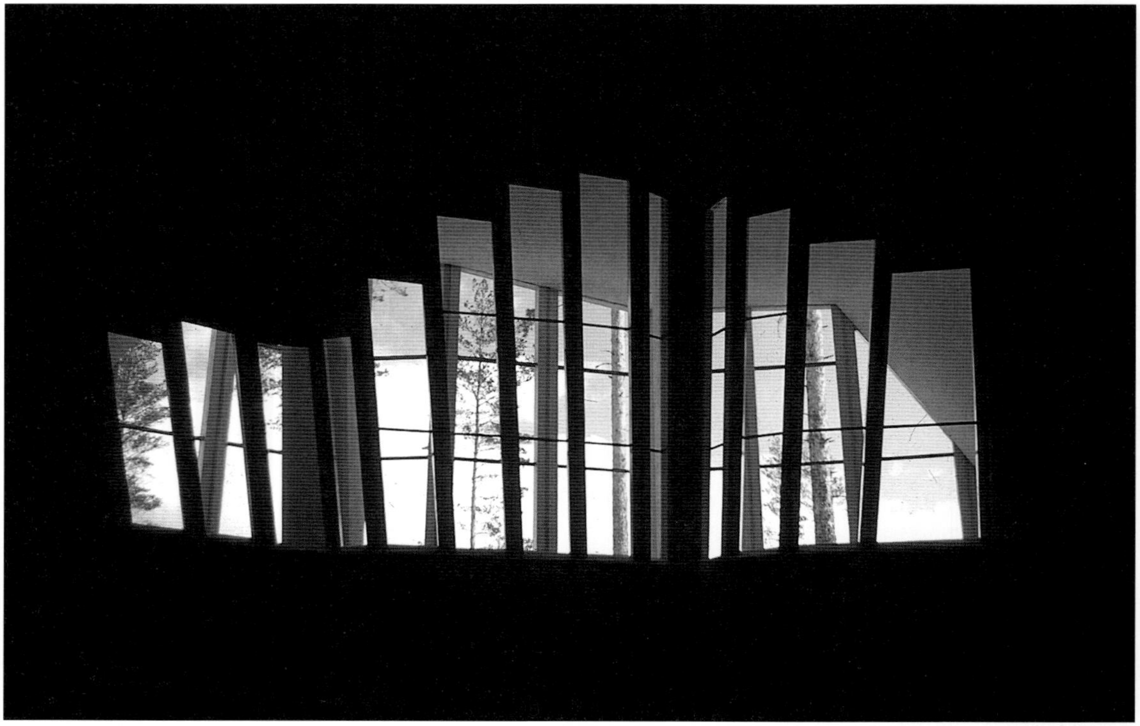

THE FINNISHNESS OF FINNISH ARCHITECTURE

Matti K. Mäkinen

But what is nature? For is custom not natural?
I am much afraid that nature is itself only
a first custom, as custom is a second nature.
Blaise Pascal

The cradle of Finnish architecture is the Finnish culture, the people in their country. Who are these Finns?

For some reason or the other, Finns are always worried about what others think of them. A group of Finnish tourists visited a zoo abroad. As an elephant was presented, the first question of the Finns was: "What do the elephants think of Finland?"

To begin with, let's take a couple of historical fragments[1]:

The Fenni live in astonishing barbarism and disgusting misery: no arms, no horses, no household; wild plants for their food, skins for their clothing, the ground for their beds.." Tacitus (c. 55–120) *Germania.*

Finlande is called a fayre countrye, because it is more pleasanter than Swecia. Much wine is transported thither, out of Spayne, by the sea Balthic, which people of the Countrye much desireth, to exhillerat their myndes...The Finnons have continual warres wyth the Muscovites in the arm or bosome of the sea Finnonicus: using in Summer the ayde of Shyppes, and in Wynther they combat upon Ice ..." George North, 1561.

What do the elephants say

And then, a jump over centuries to the present. Browsing the Internet randomly, I found pages, where some foreigners were asked about their feelings of Finland. They were people who through

[1] "Virtual Finland", an Internet presentation, 2002, The Finnish Foreign Ministry: <http://virtual.finland.fi/>

work or marriage had a longer experience of living in Finland. How had they found the people and the country, as to their expectations, experiences and other features?

– Englishman from London, teaching English in a language school:

I arrived with almost no expectations – except snow and Sibelius – the former I don't like the latter I love! At first Finns seemed very quiet – but very kind personally. Sometimes I think the Finns jump on every new trend and fashion without thinking – they have enough of their own without imitating other countries.

– German, with a Finnish husband and 3 children, lived in many countries. Had no special expectations, just following her husband.

During the years, a great change has occurred. Both Helsinki and the country is now European. Still problems in understanding the character of the people, their structures of communication. The Finns are careful in expressing opinions. The Germans are more sociable and emotional, the Finns more pragmatic and sticking to the facts. In working life, they tend to act unsupervised, they do not like to wait for orders or instructions. They avoid tresspassing the private sphere of other people. And it is difficult to adopt the rules of using first names in communication with others.

– Spaniard from Madrid, married to a Finn for 17 years.

Nature was the most significant feature of the country. Of culture, I knew Sibelius and Waltari, the author, not very much of architecture. During my first visit I found what I expected, reindeers, lakes, pine forests, the midnight sun, even some Lapps in traditional outfit. The people I found very silent and cool.

Now there has been a rapid change, the country is very European. I have learned that people here are actually not so cold; the difficulties lie in building contacts. The Finns have a strong feeling for duty; they are independent which supports their development towards the humane.

– Mexican from Mexico City, lived in Finland 1995–99, then moved to the USA.

Living in Finland was a very enriching experience. There are many cultural differences between Mexico and Finland. I love the open, honest, straight-forward and hard-working Finnish mentality. Probably, my experience was in phase of growth in technology areas where mobile technology has one of the most significant changes. Also, I experienced a lot of internationalization throughout the European Union processes on-going. I experienced Finnish people, Finland itself, and mostly Helsinki becoming more international.

And how do the Finns judge themselves?

A recent study[2] indicates that among the most important values of Finns at present are: easygoing cordiality, conformity, free opportunity for individual performance, hedonism, stimuli and impulsiveness... An interesting duality is found between the love of tradition and a pioneering radicalism. Predictable, harmonious continuity and secured future for the society, for oneself and the closest family and friends are valued high.

Finnish Architecture – box or instrument?

After this excursion to the national contexts, we can return to our topic, architecture. Why not start with the Balthusian Dilemma, so bravely explored in an earlier letter by Malcolm Quantrill.

Architecture represents the characteristics of either *a* BOX *or those of a* MUSICAL INSTRUMENT: *In the first case presenting a rigid, inflexible form, and in the second positing an open framework that permits fingering which leads to performance and interpretation". My theory examines the nature of architectural concepts in terms of their real and perceived identities... Given the choice between an inflexible, silent* BOX and the poetic, lyrical potential of an INSTRUMENT, *we may understand the architect's Balthusian Dilemma.*

Can modern Finnish architecture be characterised in terms of a box or an instrument? I – a Finnish architect myself – would not hesitate to give my vote to a box. Especially after the invasion of full glass office boxes on the most visible spots in our towns, this is the first image to pop up in the mind. Here, I can hear the angry remarks of opposition: How can you say box? Have you forgotten the frozen music of Aalto's undulating movements, Pietilä's playful counterpoints, the solemn cadences in Leiviskä's churches?

No, I have not forgotten them. But neither have I forgotten the prevailing majority, the lower upper class of our architectural everyday, where no Gehry has been duplicated to make a music hall look like a guitar, not even a concert piano. The first rule for our modern architecture seems to dwell in the silent, motionless box, in the avoidance of vibrations and gesticulations, in mute minimalism. What is the secret of such a box? Does it contain a total nothingness with nothing to say? Or will it burst open one day, spitting out all the furious spices of the market economy that have been brewing behind the transparent inpenetrability of the glass walls?

[2] Martti Puohiniemi, *Arvot, asenteet ja ajankuva* [Values, Attitudes and Picture of the Times], Dark Oy, Vantaa, 2002.

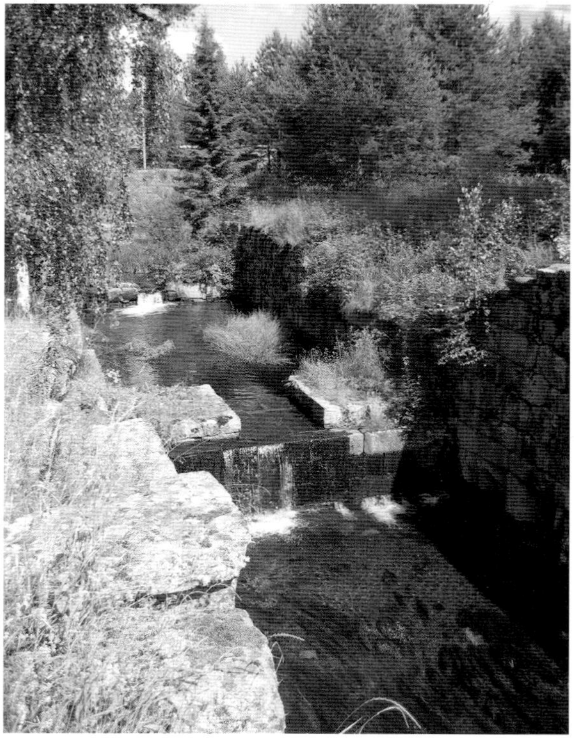

Our domestic way of building may well be what we have deserved and what we are willing to pay for. It may even give us a good night's sleep, order and predictability. For international use, we have to invest stronger condiments.

Architecture can be imported – and exported. Finnish architecture is what is designed by Finnish architects, as Kristian Gullichsen points out. A fine example of this is his new Finnish Embassy in Stockholm. Some of our embassies from recent years have proved to be successful feats in our official image-building, submitting the idea of a progressive nation somewhere beyond the seas and distant mountains. I only have to mention capitals like New Delhi, Washington DC, or Berlin where some of our most renowned embassies are located.

Previous to these years of image-building and story-telling, we have to remember the centuries of cultural interchange, where the architectural styles and practical methods of construction came to Finland as part of the cargo from east and west. As a fertilizing factor has often been noted the geographical location of this country, providing a meeting line for the Western and Byzantine cultures, including religion, architecture and the ways of everyday thinking and acting.

Architects tend to think that good architecture – whatever that means – is a natural prerequisite to a good built environment. It can be, but it need not be. Even here we meet very complicated questions of definitions. The focus, once again, is in searching for the essence of architecture. From time to time, architecture seems to avoid definitions – or alternatively, accept all of them or any of them. Observing the phenomenon, you could come to the conclusion that architecture creates and re-creates its standards through its practical applications, its paradigms in constant motion towards unknown destinations.

The changing and the sustainable

A good part of the problems in our built environment are not genuinely of Finnish origin. The delivering pains of modernity are felt here in many ways, as they are in other parts of the world. A part of the ache comes through the rapid change that hits from many directions simultaneously, suddenly, even unexpectedly. We are not mentally prepared, we feel perplexed, unsure, nostalgic and sorry.

A more optimistic way to handle the problems is to call them challenges. To name briefly only some of these common international challenges, the following themes can be mentioned:

— the growth complex, the limits of growth, the benefits and the curses of growth, what kind of growth should or could be favoured, if any? The collision with the sustainable, the impossibility and the Doomsday of continuous growth.
– the global/local interplay combined with the questions of identities, of place and placelessness, of immaterial places and fancy identities created within new cyberspaces.
– the conflicting paradigms of ecology and the free market economy, which cannot meet in a friendly way on the same planet.
– the value-crisis of architecture, where the leading trends come from the rapidly changing fashions of publicised world architecture or from the contextual ideologies mentioned above. This can lead to a Singapore phenomenon where a *tabula rasa* has replaced practically the whole community and a new history can be rapidly built on a cleared lot, if needed.

The Finnish built environment

Finally, I come to my key question: What is good and what is bad in the Finnish built environment? The world-wide issues I touched on above mainly result from the ideas of modernity, and in combination with continuous growth and the rapidly increasing degree of urbanisation provide one base and starting point for architecture, not to speak of a necessity.

In Finland, another important starting point is the interplay of the first and the second nature, nature and culture, the natural and cultural environment. In a country with a relatively low population density, with a relatively small part of the land area used for the built environment, with a history of repeated wars leading to a continuous urge for rebuilding, there has been a constant need and opportunity for re-thinking, and renewal. This situation may have played a part in the course taken by our architecture, where the intimate relation to nature and readiness for even radical acceptance of novelties has often been referred to.

This is not the time and place to embark on a deeper study of the keys to Finnish architecture. Still, I believe that they can largely be found within the circle of:

1 – the first nature (original nature) – man's first nature (human species), an imaginable archetype.
2 – the second nature (built environment) – man's second nature (culture) and architecture derived in the contexts of the second nature.

3 – the third nature (urban environment) – man's third nature (placeless globalism) and architecture developed in the contexts of the third nature (the architects' architecture, autonomous architecture, l'art pour l'art).
4 – the fourth nature (cyberspace on the web) – man's fourth nature (the avatar)[3] and architecture developed in the context of the fourth nature (cybertecture, the architecture of cybercities)

In Finland at the moment, we seem to be hovering between the stages 2 and 3, the local and the global. A final step to the third station, a whole-hearted melting into the global architectural community would end the story of Finnish architecture. Or is there a third way? Alas, this is not the full picture of the seed-bed of Finnish architecture. Along with the global trends briefly mentioned above, the third nature of Architecture, architecture built on architecture, on the ideas and paradigms of architecture and urbanism, seems to be winning ground. How it serves the various needs of mankind, is a question that deserves attention. Or does it?

Of the aching toe....

Finally, I will draft a short list of the positive and negative qualities in Finland's built environment. Let's start with some negative observations.

– lacking a sense of community
The Finns are lonely riders, our architects are lonely heroes, struggling for their place in the limelight. A humble harmonising and fitting of our works into greater entities is not our way of thinking. Maybe we are in a process of learning, though.

– lacking a sense of place
Look at our streets and squares, not the parade ones but the everyday ones. Look at the spaces between, between the roads and between the buildings. Do we have too much space to be able to refine it into places?

– lacking a sense of the large scale
Our urbanism is relatively young and the tradition of large scales is brief. Due to the repeated wars and the predominating use of timber, the history of most Finnish towns is a history of a succession of disastrous fires. Re-establishing urban culture and building urban environments has provided problems in all sectors and levels. The Finnish model town is still awaiting its time.

[3] Virtual identity

– lacking a sense of the small scale
Look at the details, if any. The carpenters' work is careless. The details are crude, often without a historical backing, haphazardly designed and executed. The mute, simple surfaces can be a trademark of "silent architecture" and, in a very few cases, they brilliantly are. Mainly though, the unarticulated clumsiness tells of haste, greed or nonchalance.

– knowing but not doing
We certainly have an idea of the ecologically, socially and culturally favourable. We can even base our planning on that knowledge. Still, our way of stubbornly building our version of the American dream with its dispersed urban structures, its obligatory automobile culture, its markets and Disneylands, is in a severe conflict with the concepts of our sustainable future.

...and some remedies

At this point of the story, for the sake of a cool balance, some positive features should be mentioned.

+ the quiet modesty of the places not touched by urban change.

+ the relatively calm simplicity of many new developments, a distant reminder of our old wooden towns in the way they once existed. One important difference, however, is that the old towns were real towns with a full variety of different functions. The quiet, friendly neighbourhoods of today, the sleeping quarters, represent only a very narrowly conceived slice of the idea of dwelling. These environments can be boring but a degree of official control guarantees a certain standard and prevents excessive demonstrations of uncultured individuality.

+ the overall standard of our built environment stands up to international comparisons fairly well, enough to make us feel too readily happy.

+ building in Finland is mainly based on real functional needs. Accordingly, the environment tells of its use and purpose. Of course, the channels of world trade and the global movement of capital open new gates for real estate speculation, and until now our peripheral location has saved us from these battles, to be fought maybe too soon in the near future.

From forester to street-wisdom

"*In literature, the greatest part consists of silence, filled up by the reader*".[4]

The minimalist approach, a silent language of architecture, even muteness, has by several critics been listed as a typical feature of Finnish architecture.

An air of silence seems to be hovering around and above the Finnish architectural scenery.

The national propaganda introducing the persons and products of our architecture has made efforts to interpret the mute silence of our architecture as a typically Finnish version of a cordial smile. The noble savage, the warm-hearted man putting his forest wisdom into practical use by inventively turning it to serve the culture.

Roger Connah has analysed the phenomenon of silence in Finnish culture, especially within the architectural institution. He opens one of his texts by mentioning some moral connotations of silence:[5]

"To believe architecture can be read as a refuge from today's stress and confusion ('generalized' loss of values, moral decay, lack of social commitment, etc.) in society (and in architecture itself), we have established its key to the logics of respite.It is a romantic notion that recalls eighteenth-century travellers seeking purity in the morals and virtuousness of the past.[6] The tradition of silence claimed from this is a further translation of refuge and virtue..."

The silence in architecture can be read – or should I say "heard" – as associations pointing as well to the past as the future. The presence can also be "heard". Just think of a row of prototypal modern office buildings involved in a mute dialogue, the full-glass walls facing each other. You sense the time stopping in the interface between the crystalline surfaces, the standing echo of reflecting and re-reflecting. What can break this magic presence and awaken the clocks?

The "silent" past imagined as an authentic life in genuine surroundings, a noble rustic simplicity with no unnecessary gestures. Of course this is all imagination, but something in our souls loves this

[4] Kristina Carlson, "Hän" [He/She], column in *Suomen Kuvalehti*, 50/1999
[5] Roger Connah: "Sometimes and Always, with Mixed Feelings: Untimely Notes on a Culture of Silence", in Malcolm Quantrill and Bruce Webb (Ed.), *The Culture of Silence. Architecture's Fifth Dimension.* College Station, Texas A&M University Press, 1998.
[6] Here Connah refers to Anssi Halmesvirta, *The British Conception of the Finnish "Race", Nation and Culture, 1760–1918.* Societas Historica Finlandiae, Studia Historica 34, Helsinki, Gummerus, 1990.

archetypal idea of "good olden times". To quote Anais Nin: "We do not see things as they are. We see them as we are." [7]

The "silent" future may not be so silent at all. The seeds of time seem to be sown to promote the opposite. On one hand, the international fashion of architecture, the way you meet it in the commercial and public buildings, is as silent, mute, closed, secured and shaded as ever. But, stronger than ever, the architecture and its makers feel a growing urge to make news, to get attention, to shock. And for that purpose, noise is cheaper than silence, even visually.

Maybe this still belongs to a post-modern era, these paradoxes in a simultaneous dialogue. Maybe there is no dialogue, no conflicting parties at all, just friendly encounters in a multi-valued reality.

Silence

Malcolm Quantrill has written an article "Breaking the Culture of Silence; or, the Case of a Talkative Finnish Architect" [8]. Roger Connah has continued his studies on silence in a comprehensive and innovative way. Many other architectural critics have also handled the theme. As a general cultural topic, the notion of silence has been widely favoured.

In writing a few lines on the Finnishness of our architecture, I cannot leave this field unnoticed.

But this is not the time and place to try a more profound approach.

As a future vision, I cannot be very wrong by claiming that even in the field of architecture, the tacit knowledge of the forest-wise Finns is in the process of turning into a tacit knowledge of streetwise Finns. And this silence goes on brewing, in material and immaterial senses, a wisdom of silent sparing of words and actions, in the theory and practice of architecture.

"A silence without meaning does not exist" [9]

[7] Anais Nin, *Seduction of the Minotaur*, Athens, OH., Swallow Press, 1961.
[8] *The Culture of Silence* edited byt Malcolm Quantrill and Bruce Webb, 1998.
[9] Hannele Koivunen, *Hiljainen tieto* [Tacit Knowledge] Helsinki, Otava, 1997.

EPILOGUE

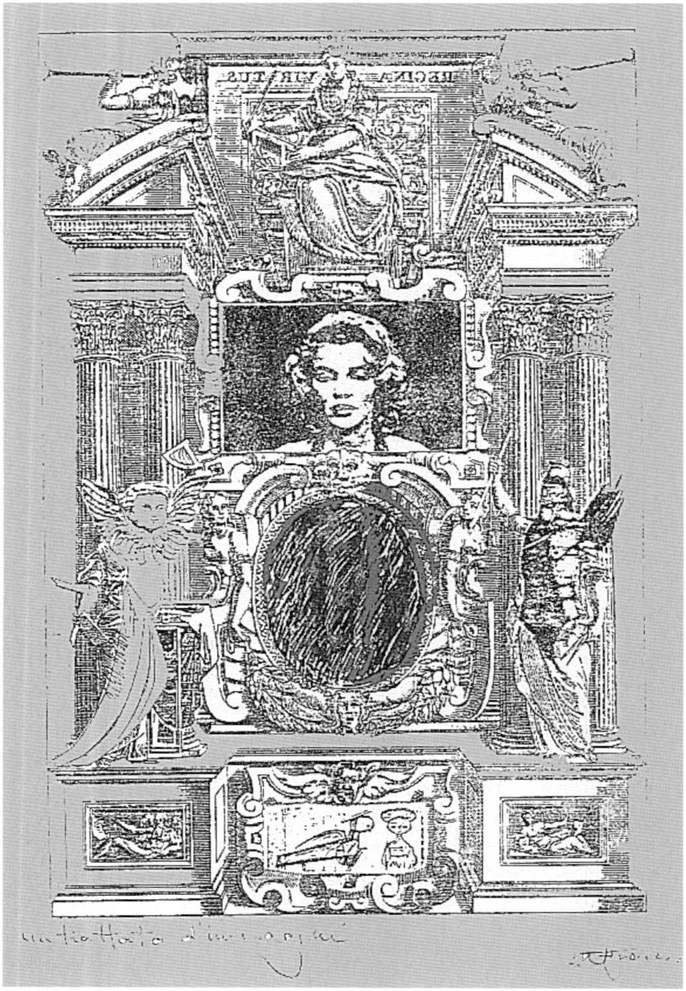
un trattato d'immagini

THE FUTURICITY OF ARCHITECTURE

Matti K. Mäkinen

Time present and time past
Are both perhaps present in time future,
If all time is eternally present
All time is eternally present
All time is unredeemable.
T.S. Eliot (*Four Quartets*, 1943)

Attempting to combine two disciplines, futures study and architecture, may give all the signals of a desperate effort. But life must go on. In spite of all the warnings of those who know better, we rig our vessel, spread the sails and leave it to the mercy of wilful winds.

John Fowles gave in the 1960s some coordinates in his personal philosophy "The Aristos" .

The Wreck and the Raft

Humanity on its raft. The raft on the endless ocean. From his present dissatisfaction man reasons that there was some catastrophic wreck in the past, before which he was happy; some golden age, some Garden of Eden. He also reasons that somewhere ahead lies a promised land, a land without conflict. Meanwhile, he is miserably en passage, this myth lies deeper than religious faith.

"Seven men inhabit the raft. The pessimist, for whom the good things of life are no more than lures to prolong suffering; the egocentric, whose motto is Carpe diem – enjoy toddy – and who does his best to get the most comfortable part of the raft for himself; the optimist, always scanning the horizon for the promised land; the observer, who finds it enough to write the logbook off the voyage and to note down the behaviour of the sea, the raft and his fellow-victims; the altruist, who finds his reason for being in the need to deny himself and to help others; the stoic, who believes in nothing but his own refusal to jump overboard and end it all; and finally the child, the one born, as some with perfect pitch, with perfect ignorance – the pitifully ubiquitous child, who believes that all will be explained in the end, the nightmare fade and the green shore rise".[1]

In our presentation here, we cannot be sure if we fit into the role of the hopeful child or some of the others characterized above. But why worry about that, out we sail…

The History of the Future

To avoid the first cliffs, we adapt the advise of some other thinkers. One of them is the English philosopher R.G. Collingwood, whose main bulk of work saw daylight in the 1930s. His interpretation of the philosophy of history has been an important inspiration for us. The meta-historical approach in his "The Idea of History" has been one of our most thought evoking sources. Following his path of thinking, we have – rather unexpectedly – come to the point of questioning.

Why try a study of the future of architecture? Why not steal a look behind the curtain and instead of a shortcut to some fancy future take use of the energy stored in history?

Why not write a History of the Future, a History of the Future of Architecture?

What sense does this make? Again, we have to return to the two elements of this study, the futures research and the architecture. We have to check the attitudes, approaches and routines of the futures researcher, as well as those of the architect, their educational backgrounds, their training, their respective professional intentions, goals and ambitions.

The futures researcher tries to analyse the future, which unfortunately is not there to be analysed. So he has to construct his future, create it as a vision, using statistics and trend extrapolations, drafting scenarios, closing his eyes and creating visions of strengths, weaknesses, opportunities and threats lurking behind the corners of his forking path.

The architect tries to find some sense in the mystery of "what is this thing called architecture". Even he tries to construct his architecture, give it a personal touch at the same time, unlike and yet so much on the lines of all the other architecture he has seen. Even he tries to make his dreams come true, and – as some architects claim they are doing – make the dreams of other people come true.

The historian tries to find out and understand events that occurred in times past. The problem is similar to that of futures studies, the subject is not present at the time of study. But the differing times

[1]John Fowles, *The Aristos. A Self-Portrait in Ideals*, Cape, London, 1964

are not the whole problem, the overall contexts might be. On the other side, the subject of futures studies can be present, available for closer studies, because so much of our future is with us already, here and now.

But let us side-step to the thoughts of R.G. Collingwood. He writes:

"Philosophy is reflective. The philosophizing mind never simply thinks about an object, it always, while thinking about any object, thinks also about its own thought about that object. Philosophy may thus be called thought of the second degree, thought about thought."

The philosopher is concerned with these events not as things in themselves but as things known to the historian, and to ask, not what kind of events they were and when and where they took place, but what it is about them that makes it possible for historians to know them.

"Philosophy cannot separate the study of knowing from the study of what is known. This impossibility follows directly from the idea of philosophy as thought of the second degree."[2]

Towards a Futuricity?

At this point, we can return to the History of the Future of Architecture. What is there about this history, this future, to make it possible for us to know it, or at least to know something of it, our thought of the thought, the way we never know the whole truth about the past history either?

Why 'historicity' instead of 'history'? Because the term 'history' suggests an objectively existing, cognitively available reality; 'historicity' implies that what we conceive of as history is tentative, situated, contingent.[3]

Do we have to speak of 'historicity'? And, accordingly 'futuricity'? This is one of the questions we'll handle in the following.

Structures – functions – meanings

In order to study a multi-disciplinary object like architecture – not to speak of studying the future – we need some organising principle. One possible way of building a framework is to use the three elements of the built environment, which in several sources are listed as the structures, functions (or activities) and meanings connected with the object. Speaking of environments, we come to the

[2] R.G. Collingwood, *The Idea of History*, Oxford University Press, Oxford, 1961 (1946)

[3] See John Lyle, "Some Post-Structuralist Assumptions", Internet presentation: http://www.brocku.ca/english/courses/4F70/poststruct.html (1997/11.3.2004).

concept of the "local" and the "place" and along with that the concept of "genius loci", the spirit of place, known already to the old Romans.

Avoiding at this stage the borderlines between the built environment and architecture, we can assume that in any built environment you can meet these three components, structures, functions and meanings. Whether a "genius loci" is always present, is a more complicated question. In our brave sailing metaphor, this threepartite list represents the body, the sails and the flags of our ship. Thus equipped, let us set out.

The structures

When speaking of structures in the context of architecture, we automatically limit our subject to the physical, material structures that make a building. In this study, the structures are understood in a more comprehensive sense. Thus we do not limit our interest to the physical framework of a building – not at all. We open our angle from the actual event of building or creating architecture to all the variety of material and immaterial structures that make the context of architecture.

One way of illustrating these contexts is shown in the short list of the main elements of 'sustainable development', a list which was given to complete and explain this concept as issued by the Brundtland Commission in the late 1980s. Accordingly, the elements of sustainable development consist of four parts, all taken into account simultaneously to justify the use of the term: the ecological, economic, social and cultural aspects of development.

Following this line of thought, sustainable development, as a precondition of sustainability in architecture, brings the material and immaterial structures of ecology, economy, social balance and culture into the sphere of considerations.

Later, we shall give a thought to the dimensions of architecture, to the boundaries between architecture and urban planning, if they can be defined. Here, we only make a hint at the 'futuricity', the future relevance of these potential elements of change, not forgetting the significance of these 'societal' factors which finally form the context for all architecture.

The Functions

Once upon the time, the functions gave the name for one important "ism" within architecture. But with or without reference to any "isms", all works of architecture, not to speak of the works of plain "building" – wherever the borderline is – are created to serve a function. In most cases, this function includes serving an activity, in some cases the practical function is mainly nominal and the symbolic value stands for the function. We build a monument, a landmark, a sign. As to the more everyday functions, we can recall Roland Barthes's statement: *"As soon as there is a society, every usage is converted into a sign of itself."* [4]

Carrying messages of the use adds remarkably to the function of any building. When the buildings 'talk', when they announce that "I am a school", "I am a church", "I am a service station", "I am a government office building", etc., they add significantly to the readability of the environment and make orientation possible. On the other hand, this provides a weak point. What happens by and by to our collective memory, when new modes of use take over, the functions of the buildings change but the old signs, the old messages, remain characterising the basic appearance? Time loses its memory-aids.

Our use of the word 'functions' here refers to two interpretations. One is the functional presence of the building itself, how it works spatially and as a physical structure. The other is the users' activities enquartered within the building, the main 'raison d'etre' for the establishment.

The Meanings

Along with any change of the structures, of the functions of a building or its users' activities, also follows a change of meanings connected with the building. And vice versa. If the meaning changes, something is bound to happen to the other two elements of the environment.

With 'meanings' we can also refer to different qualities: the building as a symbol, as a sign or message, as a fixed point of orientation, an aid for environmental readability: all of these belong to this group. Concepts like 'image', 'profile' or even 'brand' can be placed under this heading of meanings, as well as the long list of different values connected with the object.

When we say that the houses 'speak', when we study the 'language of architecture', we also mainly refer to some meaningful message attached to the built object. Or, if we want to give some nasty critique, we can quit the language of the building as meaningless babble.

[4] Roland Barthes, *Elements of Semiology*, Cape, London, 1968.

Renato De Fusco (1967) studies architecture as a mass medium. He takes the question of the language of architecture to a larger scale of society's power structures.[5] In his study of this 'metalanguage' he refers to a silent agreement between the decisionmakers and the 'masses', the users. On the one hand, a user making or accepting excentric choices runs the risk of becoming socially brandmarked, on the other hand the 'languages' emerging through decisionmaking are not uncontrollably free.

The community can exercise influence through, for example:
– the common societal development, including the new needs created by conscious marketing
– certain solutions appear or disappear due to changes in economy
– ideological or ethical factors limit the design alternatives.

Amos Rapoport states (1981) that "Meaning is not something apart from function, but is itself a most important aspect of function.... Elements of the environment do encode information that people decode." And, to make this possible, people must have a common code.

Paving the road to Futuricity

A piece of an e-mail dialogue between the authors may mark the beginning of our road to the Futuricity of Architecture.

MQ: *How do we connect with this fabric of remembrance, these memories that weave the past threads into our present fabric? The German philosopher, Hegel, hyphenated the German word for "memory" – Erinnerung as "Er – Innerung" – meaning "the inwardizing of images, experiences et cetera". In this way he sought to demonstrate how each one of us inwardizes our own favourite tales or myths, developing these into memories over time. Certain resonances are struck within us as we inwardize particular images, elements and forms, creating "models" of preferred structures, literally "an architecture of the mind".*

MKM: *Er-innerung is directed to the past, pro-videntia (foresight, caring, providence) to the future.*

Michael Wexionius, professor at the old Academy in Turku, Finland, writes that "the first rule for all human activity is to choose the good and discard the bad".

His doctor's thesis was the first thesis printed by the Academy. He continues: "the moral philosophers have given a threefold eye to the wisdom: the memory to look at the past, the understanding to see the present and the care for nurturing the future."

[5] Renato De Fusco, *Architektur als Massenmedium*, Vieweg, Wiesbaden, 1995 (1967)

John Mc Hale states *that the future of the past is in the future, the future of the present is in the past and the future of the future is in the present.*[6]

Our last guide on this time-travelling is Niklas Luhmann.[7] "*The time points out the difference between the past and the future. The time does not guarantee that something in the future will be the way it was in the past.*

In a situation where both continuity and discontinuity are possible, it depends of always new presents (and also of the presents of yesterday or to-morrow) whether continuity or discontinuity will take over. The rails of the necessary and the impossible that joined the past to the future go astray. The accepted form of standard procedure provides now an obstacle for changing structures. Innovations meet resistance, many things are technically not yet ready to be realised. But the opposition is not in the place or the time, it is rather – along with the reality – experienced as a clash between two different communications. This leads to explanations under the cover of conflicting values, interests, risks and unsatisfactory levels or knowing or cunning.

No time is content with the time, Jean Paul comments. And the irritation is worst in times where a decision must be made, pro or contra."

Following our historians' policy, we do not even dream of giving any details or painting any scenarios of the future architecture. One is for sure: the future will not be the way it used to be.

What have we been trying, then? We approach our object by checking the premises, by searching for the elements of change rather than the detailed results. We prefer the journey rather than reaching the end-station. We study the structures rather than the rivet-heads. We study the different aspects that will form and re-form the contexts of architecture to be.

The bed of Architecture is always unmade. But it carries memories of sweet dreams.

[6] John Mc Hale: The Future of the Future, George Braziller, New York, 1969
[7] Niklas Luhmann: Gesellschaftsstruktur und Semantik Suhrkamp a.M., 1995
(translation to English Matti K. Mäkinen)

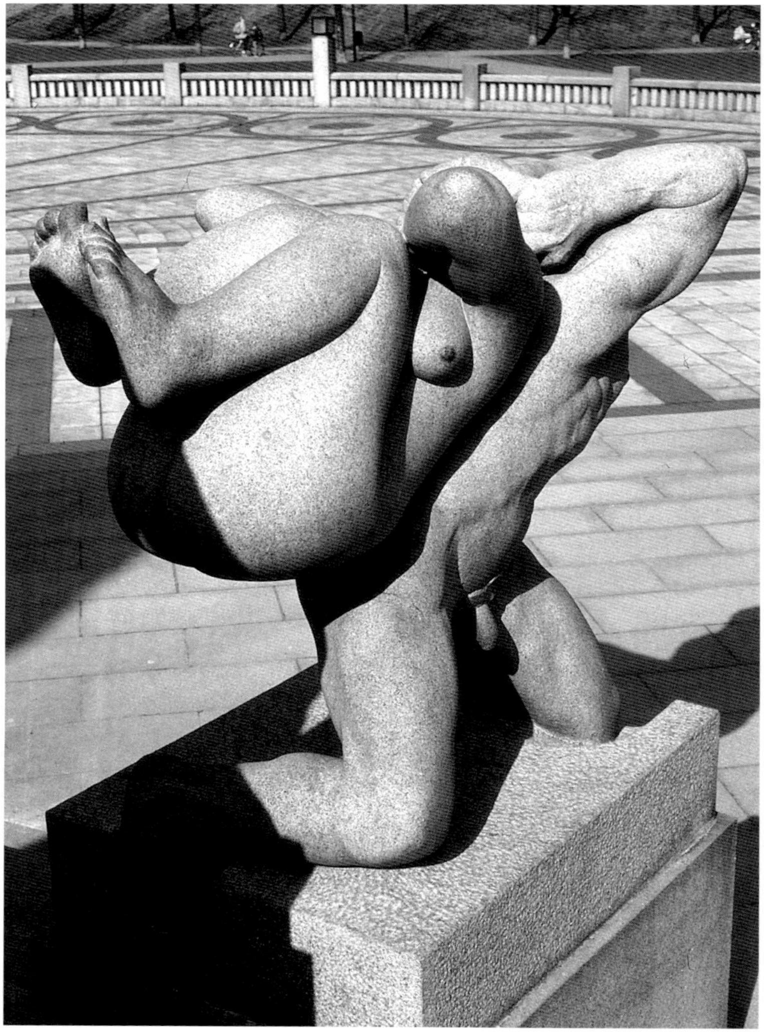

THE UNMADE BED OF ARCHITECTURE

Malcolm Quantrill

There is a sense of "the morning after" that is attached to the feelings (or lack of them?) associated with waking up with an all-too blurred memory of too much wine or whiskey having been taken on board the previous evening. We speak of being "hung-over", an expression we might accept as being valid also in architecture, the effect of being in a present *condition* that is very much dependent on some previous habits or a way of life. The "hung over" condition exhibits presence of fatigue, combined at the same time with an absence of vitality, a feeling of *deja-vu,* and an almost total lack of function in both body and mind. This could be said to apply also in certain instances with regard to architecture, most particularly where an architect is completely dependent upon historically eclectic sources, where being "hung-over" from a previous design viewpoint manifests itself in work that is essentially tired, and completely lacking in the freshness of those pristine, crisply ironed bed sheets that await the sporting entry of bride and groom.

Certainly our concern is not so much with being *hung-over* in the sense of a post-alcoholic stupor, rather the notion of an *unmade bed* here is evidence of *amorous desire* leading to *extreme pleasure* and those after-effects that are distinctly different from those of the alcoholic hang-over, for the *unmade bed* in this instance is associated with the so-called honeymoon, and the couch on which Love's designs have been made good, on which the lovers' ritual pledges have been made good, where that mere sketch design for a Love Nest has witnessed both its construction and its subsequent collapse, leaving both the lovers and their nest in some disarray. Hence, the *unmade-bed,* the couch on which the lovers' intentions have been laid bare and realized, causing those pristine sheets to succumb equally to caresses and assaults, and in consequence causing the *winding sheet,* as it were, *to come unwound.* The confusion left in the wake of the *unmade-bed* is but an abstract remnant of what architect's describe as "a question of relationships".

When the lovers leave their marriage bed, they seek a new life enlightened by the oneness they have shared *between the covers.* But they cannot just toss aside that intimacy of limbs and tongues and words and gestures which had promised an eternity of forms and sensations to fill the gaps in their former lives. Their bonding has delineated unfamiliar spaces that would accommodate an empire of voids in the world they knew before their conjugal embrace – at the same time both binding and liberating. The idea of the marital bed is a beloved project: towards it, in it, through it, the espoused couple have embraced their newly acquired conjugal rights and pursued an escape route that will release them from their old world of anticipation and anxiety, and allow them to enter instead a new realm of instant and harmonious gratification. With their ordained and ceremonial coupling behind them, they sit out on a high-perched balcony, Romeo and Juliet now side-by-side. They embrace gently, sharing the numbing aftermath of conjugal fatigue; they look out over a landscape shaped by outlines of future joys and exhilaration, allowing their eyes to wander over clumps of flowering shrubs and avenues of budding fruit trees.

Clearly, in this high-flown, blissful state, the nocturnal drama of the immediate past is but a backdrop to their enjoyment of present, fresh and wonderful pleasures. But not everything in that background can be allowed to pass without further review and comment, even requiring some remedial action on their part. For we must not forget that the ecstasy of the conjugal pair has left its mark in passing. The search for honey beneath the "Peeping Thomas" of a blinkered moon has turned the formerly smooth surfaces of love's much trumpeted playground into distinctly ruffled and dishevelled masses of sheet and comforter. The creative explorations of the wedding night have, like the creative gestures of architecture, left behind the indisputable evidence offered by an *unmade-bed.* Like the honeymooners, the architect will discover the vicissitudes of returning to a *dishevelled couch.* The forward view from a projecting balcony may be fine, but the rear-view mirror will present the architect with the haunting image of his struggles in that *unmade-bed.* And this rear-view reminder of his former life and ways must be taken into account when star-gazing or in efforts to plough new fields – or beds – projecting virgin terrain that still waits to be worked on.

One of the essays in my book *Ritual and Response in Architecture* (1974)_projected the future need for the Architect and the Client to sit on the same side of the table. This was certainly not an idea close to Frank Lloyd Wright's heart: When he was designing the Darwin Martin House (1903–1905), Mr Martin frequently sided with Wright against the wishes of Mrs Martin, but that quickly had the effect of dividing the Client into two. In any case, Wright cancelled out any advantages that might have accrued from this alliance by quarreling bitterly with Darwin Martin later in the contract. It seems that Wright could never learn from his experience with clients, and as a result his life and practise were, to all intents, turned into a perpetual *unmade-bed.*

It is difficult not to look over one's shoulder in an effort to make sense of that mess of much trampled bed linen, pretending at the same time that this unmade-bed is not so much an historic remnant of an all-consuming love affair, as a nest in which to generate a rebirth. But here is Colin Rowe trying to make a case for a kind of strictly non-linear progress:

"Rather than constantly endorse the revolutionary myth,it might be more reasonable to recognize that, in the opening years of this (twentieth) century, great revolutions in thought occurred and that profound visual discoveries resulted which are still unexplained. Rather than assume intrinsic change to be the prerogative of every generation, it might be more useful to recognize that certain changes are so enormous as to impose a directive that cannot be resolved in any individual life span."

Rowe's agenda appears to be structured along Neo-historicist lines. His proposal is, in essence, yet one more argument for making progress by going backwards. The principal danger here is that those Neo-historical prescriptions are now being represented as being contiguous with, and an extension of, the *avant-garde.*

In the early 1980s, Reima Pietilä gave voice to something quite similar. He often suggested that ideas and explorations born of Early Modernism had not all been developed to their full potential, that there was still unused creative energy to be derived from the notions of the Russian Constructivist and Czech Cubist movements in architecture; the implication of all this being that we should not altogether resist the temptation to cast a glance backwards in order to see where we are going. In other words, we should take a look in the rear-view mirror in order to see what we might encounter ahead.

But whatever past remnants or other distractions we may come upon by looking back, the result of such backward/forward perspectives will inevitably be bound up with what we already know or have known. Unfortunately, the future does not actually lie in the future, which we do not know, nor in the past, which remains a tempting side glance; it actually lies in the present, in the recollection of those tired, unravelled sheets left in the honey-mooner's love-nest. It is caught up in the crumpled fabric of memory, in the exhausted and forlorn disarray of the *unmade bed.*

In the spirit of the "backward glance", I am looking back to what I wrote about 'The Urban Locus' in the *RIBA Journal* (1975):

"Architects have been too much taught to think of buildings as independent entities, but a building is only one element in the form and structure of the city. In the past, cities evolved from a number of nodal points, through the magnetic concentration of an activity and its related spaces. Today town planning attempts, by totally inadequate techniques, to achieve what used to be the consequence of slow evolution.

Our streets are just as much 'space between buildings' (what the Germans call Zwischenraum) as are our parks and squares, yet we have come to think of them mainly as arteries for traffic and dumping grounds for parked vehicles. Drivers and passengers who merely pass through those streets in their sealed vehicular environment, or use them as a parking convenience, have no attachment to the urban landscape on which they impinge. Children can no longer play safely in neighbourhood streets, not because they are unsatisfactory play areas, but because vehicular intrusion has eroded the original function of streets as vital social links, providing not only pedestrian corridors, but also generating the recreational ventilation necessary in urban residential areas.

And what about those streets, those lost avenues of fun, what became of them? Has anything happened to restore their former virtues? Was there any effort made to bring back their vital qualities of social and recreational space, as the vital threads in the urban fabric?"

As I wrote that, almost three decades ago, plans were being drawn up in many parts of Britain with the aim of restricting the vehicular onslaught on urban spaces. The aim was to revive the distinctions necessary to define PRIVATE, SEMI-PUBLIC and PUBLIC spaces within the shared urban domain of PRIVATE/PUBLIC occupancy and use.

In my own "home town" of Norwich, for example, this intention was successfully linked to the conservation of Magdalen Street, an ancient and principal thoroughfare in the centre of the city, which was framed by an encyclopaedia of mediaeval, Georgian and Edwardian architecture. This street was restored, refurbished, and painted to express its contrasts of styles and materials. At the same time, the vehicular traffic in the area was restricted to service and essential use. This project was so successfully executed that Norwich received a National Trust Award for providing "a superb model of architectural conservation of urban historic heritage".

A group of Norwich architecture enthusiasts had managed to rescue a run-down and partially deserted area in the northern part of the city and restore its individual components to a veritable pristine condition. Magdalen Street showed how a casualty of *the past* could be massaged by a civic initiative in *the present* to create a new condition for *the future*. So, the historic City of Norwich, founded by the Romans (and we still had bits of their encircling wall) had shown itself to be not only up-to-date but had succeeded in orchestrating a veritable anthology of historic buildings. In the process they had drawn a future perspective of its former architectural urbanity and all this had been achieved in a few years, during the mid-1970s.

Unfortunately, this small triumph in the reevaluation the city's historic fabric was but short-lived. By the early 1980s, most of the revived properties had once again fallen into disrepair or ruin, and at least half of them had been gutted to make way for new commercial premises of indifferent quality. An *absolute gem* of Edwardian rubbed brickwork, a Barclay's Bank, at the junction of Saint Botolph's Street with Magdalen, that had provided the focus for the rehabilitation, was demolished together with the city's only Edwardian department store, the oldest in Norwich. Another victim was the residential enclave of Georgian houses tucked away from the street off a private courtyard, a venue well-known to me for at least a quarter century. In spite of its charm and robust detailing, Opie Court, where our family doctor's practice was located, was not a locale that I looked forward to visiting, since such occasions usually involved the ritual jabbing of an unnecessarily long hypodermic needle into either my thigh or buttocks.

But the real tragedy had no connection with either the loss of history or the loss of dignity suffered by my much-punctured rump. The trump card of the *Devil of Futuricity* (a concept that surely compounds the ruination of the city with that of the English language!) was in the construction of a 4-lane highway fly-over, soaring above the ruins of the city's Future-Past renewal. This exercise in "traffic engineering" effectively wiped out any memory of New Magdalen's revitalized past, allowing drivers to look down somewhat puzzled at a future ruined by their *precious* gain of 5 minutes in journey time. As one might have guessed, the traffic engineers had not been consulted about the vehicular restrictions imposed following the beautification of Magdalen Street, so they were damned if they would discuss their fly-over project with the designers of mere buildings,

In the end 'The Magdalen Affair' became yet another case of our poorly conceived *futurism*, coming into conflict with half-baked town planning notions intended to speed the flow of inner city traffic, when it should have been focused on slowing vehicles down! This collision inevitably converted a vision of progress into a backward glance of North Norwich that had been obscured by activity and whose supposed improvement turned out to reveal only a landscape of ruin. Thus, after a brief honeymoon period, total failure to engage the spirit of *pr bono publico* was destined to bring us back to the contemplation of the familiar disarray to be found in an *unmade bed*.

In the past, much has been made of the question concerning the architect's autonomy: is he a

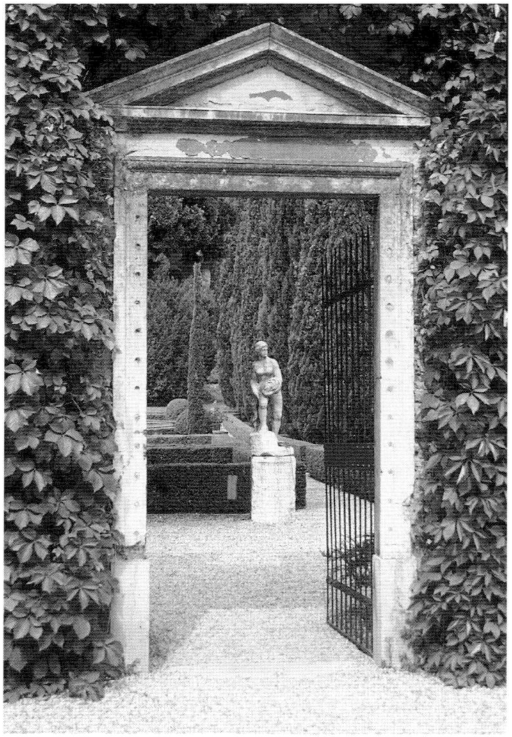

free entrepreneur, or a bonded slave of society and its institutions? According to the mythology of Ancient Greece, the originator of architecture and its culturally symbolic content was Daedalus. In addition to architectural and engineering prowess, he was appropriately renowned for his invention of tools and instruments. He was free to practice architecture in Athens until he conceived the idea of eliminating his competitor. After he was condemned for the murder of his nephew and fellow inventor, he was compelled to flee from Athens to Crete. There he continued his practice by designing the *labyrinth* for the Minotaur at Knossos. By a twist of fate, the architect's house – in this case the *labyrinth* – became his prison. In the sense that I have elaborated here, it seems that Daedalus had simply exchanged one *unmade bed* for another, both seemingly of his own making.

Is it then by some twist of fate or jig of fashion that the labyrinth has come to viewed as a model for the House of the Architect? If that's the case, this might explain the difficulty we continue to have with its ground plan.

The practice of architecture imposes an exacting range of responsibilities on both the client and the public domain, but there would appear to be two major obstacles that block the effective practice of *Baukunst.* Those are: (1) the Myth of Autonomy, or quasi-independence, which is based on an outmoded view of the architect as artist *rather than poet*; generated by misinterpretations of Italian Renaissance practice. And in spite of transformations in architecture since 1750, it still prevails to the detriment of understanding the architect's true role in society. And (2) the structure of architectural education, where, even in the wake of shifts in emphasis at the Bauhaus, at Ulm, and in Britain and the United States, has not yet found a *new regulation.* The consequence is a lack of agreement between schools, or between schools and the profession, on what constitutes a *common and appropriate body of knowledge.* And what sort of *futuricity* does that offer us? What kind of plan for a *future city* of architecture are we likely to find in that *unmade bed?*

In his *Intentions in Architecture* (1962), Christian Norberg-Schulz observed: "*It seems natural to take architecture as the point of departure for architectural education. But, as far as we can tell, this has never actually been done.*"

His statement provokes two simultaneous responses: (1) it identifies an urgent need to search for the true nature of professionalism in architecture; and (2) it provokes the need to question the continuity of discontinuous connections between the whole concept of the art of building – *Baukunst* – and an understanding of professionalism that appears to be available to students only through *unstructured gaps* in their education.

By the mid-1960s, architects had begun to embrace a new pseudo-science called "Design Methods", orchestrated mainly by non-architects who, nevertheless, claimed to support Norberg-Schulz's line of enquiry. The Design Methodists did not, however, offer any new visual order to replace "the old devalued styles". This probably accounts for Norberg-Schulz's confusion of the *means* with the *ends*? His proposal was that, henceforth, architecture should not be considered as a "separate entity", but as an embodiment of separate but related *concerns*. Nevertheless, "the work of architecture is to occupy the centre of our investigations ... a human product that requires us to investigate the conditions under which it is generated and becomes physically manifest".

To take architecture as the point of departure for architectural education, as Norberg-Schulz suggests, certainly implies "contact with reality". But I must repeat an earlier question here, namely: "What is *architecture*? What are its functional and cultural origins? How do you make it? Is it like cooking, where you have a recipe that includes (1) the ingredients; and (2) detailed procedural instructions? Or is it like poetry, a blend of ideas and feelings, forms and flavours? And what about *reality*? – Does that imply a *known context,* a set of situations or conditions, with which we have *contact* or perhaps *renewed contact*? Or is it a *changing context* that we are dealing with here? The fascination of architecture is precisely that it generates many such difficult, sometimes unanswerable, questions.

If we are talking about progress, the concept of moving forward, even if that involves swimming against the tide, we can understand that the advent of Modernism encouraged architects to abandon the eclecticism of historic styles. Instead, they were challenged to practice an abstract expressionism that reflected some of the characteristics of Post-Paxtonian industrial forms. Unfortunately, modernist architects confused the meaning of style with that of problem-solving, promoting it as a kind of patent-medicine intended to provide remedies and cures for social ills.

There is a German saying: *Form ist nicht nur Formalität* ("Form is not only formality"). It comes from the nineteenth century Viennese physician and playright, Arthur Schnitzler, and it describes precisely one of the fundamental difficulties of Modern architecture, particularly architecture of the Post-Machine Age. This problem centres on our inability to comprehend the changing relationship between art and architecture in the twentieth century. During this period Modernism in architecture has persistently attempted to interpret the style language of painters, emphasizing *image and appearance* at the expense of *content and substance.*

As Alfonso Corona-Martinez has pointed out in *The Architectural Project* (CASA, 2003) the architectural drawing that is prepared on a drafting table, perpetuates the *dessin* (drawing) relation between art and architectural design. The fact that the screen of the computer is vertical, unlike the horizontal drafting table, should help eliminate any similarity between the outmoded drafting board and the painter's redundant easel. But I can hear Norberg-Schulz cautioning from the next room: "As far as we can tell this has not actually happened!" And for this reason even the most casual sidelong glance at computer-generated graphics reveals that the designer is still looking backwards, still languishing in that *unmade bed of architecture.*

A few months after my introduction to Finland, to the sauna and my first meeting with Alvar Aalto, Lewis Mumford came to Liverpool University and gave a lecture in the Department of Civic Design. I remember him as statuesque, an impression reinforced by his heavy tweed suit, with its belted jacket and generous pocket flaps. He spoke about some monuments of Modern architecture, focusing mainly on the work of Frank Lloyd Wright and Richard Neutra. But the real theme of his lecture centred on his abhorrence of glass architecture. Reviewing Ludwig Mies van der Rohe's Farnsworth House in Illinois and Phillip Johnson's House at New Canaan, Connecticut, he asked his audience: "Who wants to live in the display window of a Main Street store? Who wants to be show-cased like an Amsterdam whore? When it comes down to it, who wants to make love in a glass-box living room?"

At question time, which followed, Paul Ritter, one of our most aggressive students, asked Professor Mumford: "Sir, do you always make love in the living room"? In response, Mumford summoned up his full height and presence, his tweeds bristling masculinity, and pronounced: "My dear young man, I have made love in every kind of room." What was important was not that we should accept his boast as truthful, but that we were inspired by his heroism, by this sure-fired and irrepressible American sexuality. A robust and confident man in his 60s, exuding that rough-hewn masculinity we normally saw only in American movies. But in reality, his splendid words had only ruffled the sheets of Architecture's unmade bed. He was a saint for us students. But, in spite of his histrionics, that bed, like Mumford himself, remained a mess of passionate intent and intellectual pretence. As the French have it: "Plus ca change, plus ca la meme chose!"

MATTI K. MÄKINEN is an author, critic, a retired administrator and university professor. Born in Helsinki, Finland, he studied at the University of Technology in Helsinki. After a successful career as an architect together with his position as director of various large architectural and engineering offices, he has been teaching at all three schools of architecture in Finland, as well as lecturing in several other countries. As Director General of The National Board of Public Building (Rakennushallitus) from 1985 to 1994, he was the last in a line of distinguished architects to hold that office. Rakennushallitus (1811–1995) was the central national agency responsible for the design, building and maintenance of Government buildings.

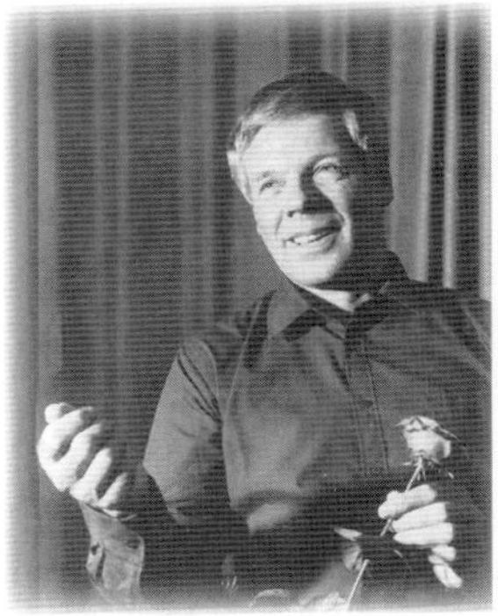

Professor Mäkinen is a former President of The Finnish Association of Architects (SAFA) and an Honorary member of Architects' Associations both in the USA (FAIA) and in Hungary (Hon MÉSZ). He has won a number of prizes in architectural competitions and has been both a member and chairman of several architecture competition juries in Finland and abroad. He was awarded the National Award for Architecture (1978) in addition to other domestic and international distinctions. Professor Mäkinen has had several books and numerous articles published on architecture and urban design, and has actively participated in public debate on planning and building matters in general.

MALCOLM QUANTRILL is internationally known as an author, teacher and critic. Born in Norwich, England, he studied architecture at the universities of Liverpool, Pennsylvania and Wroctaw and has held appointments at a number of British and American universities. In addition he has been Visiting Professor at the University at Illinois in Chicago (1974), Technische Universität, Vienna (1975–77) and the Carleton University in Ottawa (1978); and Professor of Architecture and Urban Design in the University of Jordan (1980–83). Since 1986 he has been the Distinguished Professor of Architecture at Texas A&M University. He is the Director of the Centre for the Advancement of Studies in Architecture (CASA) at the University and Co-editor of the *CASA Studies in Architecture and Culture.*

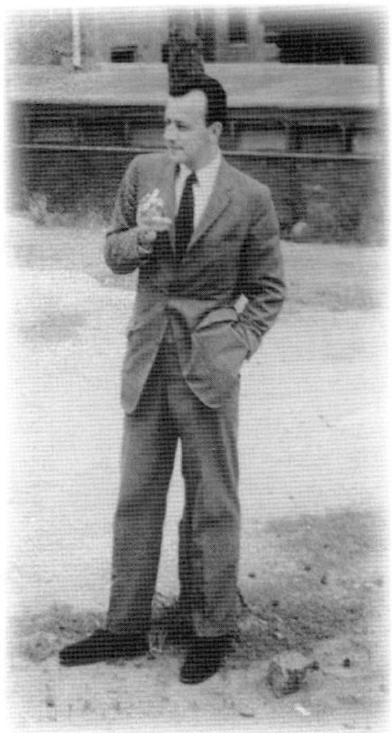

Quantrill at Otaniemi in 1957, photo Helena Ilmiökorpi

Professor Quantrill's interest in Finnish architecture began with his first visit to Finland in 1953 and he has been a serious student of modern Finnish architecture since he worked in the office of Aarne Ervi in 1959–60. He has established himself as a leading authority on the work of Alvar Aalto, lecturing widely on that subject in the United States, Europe and Australia. His books on Finnish architectural history and theory include: *Alvar Aalto: A Critical Study* (1983 and 1987); *Reima Pietilä: Architecture, Context and Modernism* (1985); *Finnish Architecture and the Modernist Tradition* (1995); *The Culture of Silence* (co-edited with Bruce Webb, 1998) and *Juha Leiviskä and the Continuity of Modern Finnish Architecture* (2001). Quantrill's contributions to Finnish culture were first officially recognized in Finland in 1988, when the Finnish President inducted him into the Order of the Lion of Finland as a Knight Commander.